*Twayne's United States Authors Series*

Sylvia E. Bowman, *Editor*

**INDIANA UNIVERSITY**

*Booth Tarkington*

# BOOTH TARKINGTON

### By KEITH J. FENNIMORE
*Albion College*

 238

Twayne Publishers, Inc.  ::  New York

**Library of Congress Cataloging in Publication Data**

Fennimore, Keith J.
    Booth Tarkington.
    (Twayne's United States authors series, TUSAS 238)

    Bibliography: p.
    1. Tarkington, Booth, 1869–1946.
PS2973.F4                    813'.5'2                    73-16403
ISBN  0-8057-0715-8

MANUFACTURED IN THE UNITED STATES OF AMERICA

To Jean Joy

# Preface

The literary status of Newton Booth Tarkington has been a persistent problem for his critics. At present, whatever his literary successes in the past (and they were many) and whatever his former critical position may have been (and it was high), Tarkington is the subject of deep silence among the academicians. The late Van Wyck Brooks remarked in *The Writer in America*, "Let the best writer cease to produce for a decade and he is as dead as mutton to the critical eye, for no one continues to cherish all the good work he may have done, no one respects the finest outmoded author."[1] Undeniably, critical standards have changed during the two generations since Tarkington arrived on the American literary scene, and popular tastes have shifted even more drastically. As Tarkington himself commented, "By our own yardsticks we select and judge the great of the past; and every succeeding period builds up certain dead artists, kicks down certain others."[2]

It is not for us to conjecture what Tarkington's ultimate position in the annals of American literature will be. At the time of Tarkington's death in 1946, one columnist in the *Saturday Review of Literature* observed that "future historians will not set him among the titans, but they will not ignore him." Now, nearly three decades later, this study is not intended to raise Booth Tarkington upon some shaky pedestal of literary eminence; rather, it strives to be a balanced assessment of his strengths and weaknesses, his virtues and vices. Special effort has been made to point out the autobiographical, philosophical, and professional significance of his major novels in relation to the social, economic, and literary climate that surrounded him.

There are several reasons why Tarkington's artistic role has suffered such uncertainty, all of which are major concerns in this study. The first was his adherence to a constant attitude toward basic aspects of literature. At the turn of the century, he emerged upon an American literary scene which was undergoing multiple changes. Finding early a congenial environment in Howellsian Realism, he rarely departed from it for nearly half a century. As a result, he repeated themes, settings, and characters into an era inimical to such subjects and alien to his own taste and talent. Most significantly, during the two generations following his first publications, the literary tides brought about profound changes in the critical standards which then and now define excellence.

Social themes, in particular, figured prominently in Tarkington's growth as a novelist. After returning to the United States from extensive foreign travel, the mature author became increasingly aware of the societal issues created by rampant industrialism. While deploring "the turmoil" of its maturation problems, Tarkington became a practical idealist who envisioned a gradual merging of tempered materialism and enlightened capitalism which would result in a progressively higher standard of living for all.

As one might expect, Tarkington also became concerned about the same sorry state of American culture which distressed "the sad young men" of the 1920's who sought artistic refuge on the Left Bank in Paris or in its Greenwich Village counterpart. Never an expatriate, despite his *Wanderjahre*, Tarkington sought to exemplify the exercise of native talent to produce a literature worthy of the finest mind, yet appealing to the general reader. Here, too, he felt paternalistic capitalism could make its contributions by unobtrusively supporting the creative artist and by making the American cultural heritage available to the broad public.

Because of Tarkington's reluctance to accept the new order in literary, moral, and social matters, he has been labeled an "unregenerate" by his peers and relegated to literary limbo. Ironically, by his own standards, Tarkington *was* a rebel—a rebel against what he considered to be a distressing attack upon formalism and taste in modern literature, an alarming invasion of morality during the Flapper Age, and a depersonalization of the individual in a mechanized society. Though willing to concede that "the world does move," he never confused change with progress. The role of the conservative in a time of liberalization is not a happy one, however; and the literary status of Tarkington has suffered materially because of his seeming intransigence.

In spite of the growing rift between Tarkington and the *literati*, grass-roots America welcomed his words to the close of his prolific career. Because of Tarkington's voluminous productivity, this relatively brief critical analysis cannot pretend to include all of some three dozen novels, another two dozen plays, plus an uncounted number of short stories and articles. By common consent among critics and readers alike, however, Tarkington's efforts in the first category—the novel—merit primary attention; hence, we concentrate our efforts upon Tarkington the novelist.

Undoubtedly Tarkington would have approved such a decision, for he too regarded the novel as the highest form of literary art. In practice, he found the short story a hospitable arena in which to flex his talents; in like manner, his juvenile writings are episodic in structure, with each segment a fairly complete tale in itself. So far as the plays are concerned, Tarkington restricted his theatrical enterprises to shrewd adaptations of his own novels or to rollicking "comedies of manners" which added much to his purse but little to his luster. In the final analysis, it was the novel by which he sought to make his mark in lasting letters.

As a result of our efforts to minimize the man (so far as mere biography is concerned) and to maximize the novelist (so far as his principal works are concerned), a more regrettable sacrifice was inevitable. The intimate details of his life have been omitted with real reluctance; for Tarkington was an engaging personality. Like Mark Twain, he left only a now-and-then autobiography. Fortunately, however, a wealth of correspondence and other records remain which already has been tapped to portray the charm, the humor, the kindness of the man.

Surely it is not without significance that a new generation is looking backward with mounting interest to the very years when Tarkington, the artist, developed those talents which won him two Pulitzer Prizes and the sobriquet "Dean of American Letters." Although separated by fifty years of chaos and change, the 1970's are discovering a closer kinship to the 1920's than anyone would have suspected a mere decade ago. In the ongoing search for lasting values of solid worth, perhaps the time will come when more will be interested in the man behind the "deanship." Certainly, it is already time to reassess his position in the hierarchy of American literature.

KEITH J. FENNIMORE

*Albion College*

# Acknowledgments

The composition of *Booth Tarkington* was expedited greatly by the efforts of Dorothy R. Russo and Thelma L. Sullivan in preparation of *A Bibliography of Booth Tarkington, 1869–1946*, copyright 1949 by the Indiana Historical Society. An even greater indebtedness for helpful insight and generous support must be accorded James Woodress, author of *Booth Tarkington: Gentleman from Indiana*, copyright 1955 by J. B. Lippincott.

Acknowledgment also is made to Russell B. Nye, Professor of English at Michigan State University, whose steady direction and perceptive advice made possible the early draft of this study.

A few words of appreciation must be given the librarians and staff of both the Albion College and the Michigan State University libraries for their indefatigable labors in securing fugitive material and patient compliance with innumerable requests.

I am particularly grateful to Albion College for granting me a semester sabbatical to work on the project; to my sister-in-law, Marion M. Livingston, for proofreading the final copy; and especially to Sylvia Bowman for the constructive editing which the manuscript required at every stage of composition. I reserve my final words of gratitude for my wife; without her constant encouragement and unstinting labor, I am sure that this book would never have seen print.

# Contents

# Chronology

1869  Newton Booth Tarkington born, July 29, Indianapolis, Indiana.

1876  Tarkington family moves into "the new house" on North Pennsylvania Avenue, Booth's home for the next forty-six years.

1881-  Begins composing tales and playlets indicative of later ro-
1882  mances and juvenilia.

1887-  After being a truant while a junior in Shortridge High School,
1889  Tarkington is withdrawn from public school. Completes preparatory education with two rewarding years at Phillips Exeter Academy.

1890  Enrolls for one year at Purdue University, dividing his interests among academic studies, art lessons, the Sigma Chi fraternity, and romance.

1891-  Completes college career as "special student" for two years
1893  at Princeton. Ineligible for degree, he majors in extracurricular activities: the Glee Club, campus publications, and theatrical enterprises.

1893-  Serves six years of literary apprenticeship, striving vainly for
1898  acceptance as fictionist and/or dramatist. Writes *Monsieur Beaucaire, The Gentleman from Indiana*, numerous plays and short pieces. Publishes nothing.

1893  Hamlin Garland accepts *The Gentleman from Indiana* for serial publication in *McClure's Magazine*. Visits New York City to revise manuscript; returns home "almost a hero." Begins adaptation of *Monsieur Beaucaire* for stage.

1900-  *Beaucaire* opens October 7 in Philadelphia. Tarkington con-
1901  tinues to write historical romance, *The Two Vanrevels*.

1902  Tarkington marries Louisa Fletcher on June 18. Returns from honeymoon to find himself Republican nominee for State Representative; elected November 5.

1903-  From January through March, fulfills office in General As-
1904  sembly. Incurs typhoid fever at French Lick; recuperates at Kennebunkport, Maine; compelled to resign from politics; embarks with family on Grand Tour of Europe.

1905  Periodical publications expand; *Harper's* serializes *The Conquest of Canaan*. Returns to Capri with Harry Leon Wilson to collaborate on plays.

| | |
|---|---|
| 1906-<br>1907 | Laurel, Tarkington's only child, born in Rome on February 11.<br>Removes to Paris; writes *His Own People* and *The Guest of Quesnay*. Returns to New York for production of *The Man from Home*. |
| 1909 | Tarkington's mother dies on April 17. Marriage problems develop. |
| 1910-<br>1911 | Tarkington drifts toward alcoholism and literary decline. Divorce from Louisa granted November 13, 1911. |
| 1912 | Year of recovery: overcomes drinking problem; regains love of writing; produces *The Flirt*; marries Susanah Robinson, November 6. |
| 1913 | First installments of *Penrod* begin lucrative career as juvenile fictionist. |
| 1914 | Writes *The Turmoil*, first of the *Growth* trilogy. |
| 1915 | Serializes *Seventeen* in *Metropolitan Magazine*. |
| 1917 | After publishing *Gentle Julia*, resumes study of urban problems created by industrialization. |
| 1918 | Writes *The Magnificent Ambersons* (awarded Pulitzer Prize the following year). |
| 1921 | Publishes *Alice Adams* (perhaps his finest novel and winner of a second Pulitzer Prize). Peak period of both creative powers and fame. |
| 1923 | Year of bereavement: Tarkington's father dies in January; his daughter, Laurel, the following April. |
| 1924 | Publication of *The Midlander* completes the *Growth* trilogy. |
| 1925-<br>1930 | After another European junket, Tarkington returns to write *The Plutocrat* and *Claire Ambler*. Serious eye problems develop. |
| 1931 | Final cataract operation marks a long period of gradual retirement. |
| 1933-<br>1941 | Through Depression years, seeks social themes in works like *This Boy Joe* and *The Heritage of Hatcher Ide* to express faith in "the American way." |
| 1946 | After surviving World War II and the opening of the Atomic Age, Tarkington dies on May 19, 1946. |

CHAPTER *1*

# The Awakening Years

FOR the late Bernard DeVoto, the proper figure for study in American letters is a man "whose thought and emotions are played upon by many forces of the age in which he lived, whose life is intricately affected by the social and economic and intellectual experiences of his time, whose books record something of the process by which the mind acts on the substance of history, whose literary significance cannot be isolated from his social significance."[1] Newton Booth Tarkington represents an almost ideal figure to set within DeVoto's framework. Born but four years after the close of the Civil War, Tarkington spent his childhood in the difficult days of the Reconstruction, his boyhood in the "Gilded Age," and his early manhood in what a forgetful posterity still calls the "Gay Nineties." His mature years felt the cataclysms of two world wars, a major depression, and the birth of the Atomic Age. Most of what we today label the marks of "progress" in such areas as communication, transportation, and manufacturing, he witnessed in every stage of development. Most of what we call "modern" in art, music, literature—even in morals and mores—he watched in its growth.

Fortunately for American letters, Tarkington did more than watch: he recorded a goodly share of these changes one way or another in his writings. As James Woodress, his most recent biographer, observes, Tarkington "pursued life intensively as long as his health permitted and observed it acutely after he was forced to the sidelines."[2] Writing near the close of Tarkington's extended career, fellow novelist John P. Marquand commented in frank admiration: "In all of his rather stupendous career he has never faltered; he has never been 'dated.' He

17

has started with the horse-and-buggy age, but manners and eccentricities, even when they ride in stream-line motors, have never left him staring bewildered and defeated through the dust. He has been able through every decade to change his models and his tools."[3] Significantly, both Henry Steele Commager (in an article on "The Rise of the City") and Lewis Atherton (in *Main Street on the Middle Border*) use *The Magnificent Ambersons* by Tarkington as their point of reference in discussing the urbanization of the Midwest.

We do not imply, however, that Tarkington merely sketched panoramic views of American life in photographic detail. To use Henry James's phrase, Tarkington drew largely from "the deep well" of his own experiences and observations. In his home town of Indianapolis, he knew firsthand the sooty smoke of Big Business and the creeping blight of the Inner City. Throughout the *Growth* trilogy and a dozen more titles, Tarkington wrote of his community with the intensivism of a William Dean Howells. Poignant in drama and rich in detail, Tarkington's studies of Midwestern industrialization in the early decades of the twentieth century constitute one of his most significant contributions to American social literature.

From broad depiction of the contemporary socio-economic scene, Tarkington frequently turned to probing the intricacies of "the feminine mystique." By some literary osmosis still obscure to his critics, Tarkington gained insights into the ways of women which provided him resources for a variety of female studies. Although surrendering at times to the charms of his own creations, Tarkington at his best displayed his subjects in the full glare of truth, winning both critical acclaim and a loyal readership for his honesty.

To the youthful reader, of course, Tarkington was the writer *par excellence* of juvenile fiction—and to many even today he may be known best for *Penrod,* for *Seventeen,* and for other tales of childhood through adolescence. Lifted largely from memories of his own boyhood and observations of his three nephews and their friends, these stories are full of rueful humor and unexpected pathos. Tarkington obviously enjoyed himself while writing about Penrod and his cohorts, and many an adult no doubt shared his enjoyment. Even today these pages speak nostalgically of a lost chapter in the history of American childhood.

In the final analysis, however, Tarkington's niche in his native letters should probably be superscribed "Social Critic." Despite his extensive forays into divergent areas, the mature artist held a steady grasp upon the shifting scenes about him. As E. S. Martin observed in his comments on Tarkington's *The World Does Move* (1928), "The attraction of Mr. Tarkington's remarks in this book and of his books in general is that while he is full of humor and ministers to entertainment and is a storyteller and sees to it that his stories are readable, in the back of his mind he is a serious man, examining life with a deeper comprehension of its processes and proceedings than any other American writer now successfully implicated in the production of works of fiction. That is why one cares to listen to him speculating about the purposes and the probable outcome of what is going on."[4]

## I  *The Tarkington Family*

Ample evidence exists to account for both Tarkington's interest in the social world about him and his early identification among "the gentility" in the world of literature. He arrived "with a minimum of inconvenience" in the early hours of July 29, 1869. His father, John Tarkington, was a lawyer of thirty-seven years who owned his own home in the better section of Indianapolis. Although Tarkington's father was the son of a zealous Methodist circuit rider during the pioneer days of Indiana—and one who subscribed to much of his own father's strict code of duty and honor—he was, from all accounts, a kind, generous man. James Woodress reports that "his humanity and gentleness undoubtedly formed his son's most characteristic traits."[5] No better evidence of Mr. Tarkington's sympathetic understanding could be offered than his patient forbearance during young Booth's apprentice years.

Booth's mother's character provided marked contrast to that of his easygoing father. Born of sturdy New England stock that traced its lineage to the first settlers of Connecticut, Elizabeth Tarkington was an assertive, dynamic woman who provided much of the driving force for the entire family. Because the best school in her home town of Terre Haute was a Catholic one, her independent Presbyterian father sent her there—and Elizabeth later did precisely the same thing for her daughter Hauté. Obviously Elizabeth Tarkington was intensely family conscious, for both her children were named after her immediate relatives. Because she was far better educated than most matrons in Indianapolis, Elizabeth brought to the Tarkington home a refinement which Booth never lost. As Woodress observes, "Her legacy to her son was not in temperament but in intellectual equipment and a cultivated taste."[6]

Tarkington's older sister, Hauté, possessed the happy knack of entering her brother's life in a series of opportune moments. Although eleven years his senior, she had unbounded affection for him and unlimited confidence in his abilities. Booth as a child dictated to Hauté his first adventure tales; and, through a long, rewarding relationship, she defended his first novel in person in the editorial office, maneuvered the arrangements which enabled the neophyte novelist to escort William Dean Howells about on a lecture visit, and salvaged her brother from incipient alcoholism.

Perhaps brief mention should also be made of Tarkington's uncle, Newton Booth, the sole "great man" on either side of the family. In true Horatio Alger fashion, he went to California in 1851 and made his fortune. Shortly after he was elected governor of the state in 1871, he was sent to the United States Senate. Partly because of his wealth, partly because he was an unmarried, doting uncle, but mainly because he bore great affection for his sister and her family, Newton exerted a frequent influence over the Tarkington household. When Booth was but three, he went with his mother and sister to visit the new dignitary; when the depression of 1893 nearly crushed John Tarkington, Newton Booth came to the rescue; when his favorite nephew was withdrawn from the public school, Uncle Newton contributed to his namesake's support at Phillips Exeter Academy; and while the would-be author was struggling to find himself, a legacy from Uncle Newton gave the young man modest financial independence. From the record, it is abundantly clear that the Tarkingtons, each and all, owed much to Newton Booth.

## II  *Youthful Exposure to Literature*

Although a wealth of delightful family anecdotes about Booth's formative years exists, for our purpose brief mention can be made only of incidents which contributed toward his writing career. These began with Tarkington as a child, for he displayed from his early childhood a persistent interest in both literature and history. Never athletic in build nor aggressive in nature, Booth the youngster soon turned from playground activities to the resources of his father's library. Nearly every day someone in the family read to him, his mother or Hauté in the afternoon, his father in the evening. The list of his preteen favorites may suggest the high level of these youthful literary experiences. From his father, for example, he absorbed Sir Walter Scott's *Tales of a Grandfather*, and "during the summer he was nine he gladly cut his play each afternoon to listen to his mother read Francois Guizot's *History of France*."[7] In fact, from his own record we learn that "while still a schoolboy, he devoured Shakespeare, histories of England and the United States, and a miscellaneous procession of novels"[8] by Scott, Charles Dickens, Victor Hugo, Wilkie Collins, Oliver Goldsmith, and others.

But Tarkington also encountered the heroes of the ten-cent thrillers which were popular during his youth. Just as youthful Penrod scribbled "The Adventures of Harold Ramorez" in the privacy of the stable sawdust box, so did preschool Tarkington dictate his tales of California gold fields to a patient sister and begin writing while barely in grammar school his own stories on the same theme. During the year 1882, when only thirteen, he kept a diary—the first of innumerable journals and copybooks in which he scribbled and sketched most of his life. When Tarkington entered his teens, he discovered a new interest which persisted nearly fifty years. Theater-going and play-reading at home had long been popular entertainment for all the Tarkington family (except for Grandfather Joseph Tarkington, the dour Methodist preacher), but young Booth set out to produce his own creations. His first effort, a fourteen-act melodrama entitled "Jesse James," was based on the current exploits of the then-famous outlaw.

When Booth's carriage-house audience approved of "Jesse James," the budding playwright-producer-actor responded while in high school with an unnamed, unfinished comedy of manners which used much of the same "country bumpkin who out-slicks the city-slickers" theme which he later developed so successfully in such favorites as *The Country Cousin* and *The Man from Home*. Both at preparatory school and at Princeton, Tarkington exploited his flair for dramatics; and he maintained even during summer vacations his zeal for everything theatrical. Far into his literary career he was rarely more happy than when he was engrossed in some aspect of play production, despite the fact that his efforts did not always produce the happiest results. The astounding success of *The Man from Home* (1908), for example, kept him away from fiction for several years while he struggled in vain to duplicate his feat.

Critic Malcolm Cowley frankly concedes that "we don't know what it is that makes a writer and gives him his curious belief in the magic of words or his notion that producing good verse or prose is something more essential than succeeding in business or winning a political campaign." According to Cowley's own explanation, however, "the future writer will have been a great reader, with his nose always in a book. At some period . . . he will have been a lonely child, forced to depend for entertainment on his inner resources. . . . Then comes a third circumstance that helps him to choose his calling when he finds that his skill in using words and making up stories enhances his status."[9] Tarkington's formative years conform almost perfectly to Cowley's three-point pattern. As noted above, young Booth was an avid reader; thanks in part to a protective mother, he was often a lonely child; and, as we have seen, he did crave status both within and without the family. Although this simple formula by no means tells the whole tale, it may be useful in pointing out some of the salient features behind Tarkington's writing career.

### III   *Belated Interest in the Academic*

Early, however, the lonely years for the boy were over. During his junior year of high school, Booth became involved in a prolonged truancy which resulted in his transference the following fall to Phillips Exeter Academy. There, for the first time, he found himself free from parental supervision, and he realized later that Exeter was the experience that "began to open his eyes to the world." After his public-school fiasco, he so successfully recouped his academic standing that his first grades showed him to be only ten points below the top of the class. More important, he was learning to associate with all types of people, to make friends—and to keep them. Most important, he maintained his literary interests by taking a succession of English courses, by engaging in "perpetual bull-sessions," and by serving as one of the editors of the class yearbook.

Next came the well-packed academic year of 1890–91 at Purdue University. Tarkington had followed a pretty girl and a gifted art instructor to Lafayette, Indiana, only to lose both by the end of the first semester. Nevertheless, he salvaged much from the year: close fellowship with Sigma Chi brothers, humorist George Ade and cartoonist John T. McCutcheon, a news column written for the home-town paper, contributions to college publications, the title role in a campus production of Gilbert and Sullivans' *Tom Cobb,* and membership in the Irving Society (an oratorical club). His greatest worry was money, for already the tightening economy of an imminent depression was making itself felt. In the spring, Tarkington wrote his mother: "You must give up the idea of Princeton. I must go to work. I have several grey hairs and enough education. If I am ever to be anything, it is time I commenced being."[10]

Money problems notwithstanding, Booth attended Princeton in the fall. Because of his deficiency in Classical languages, Booth enrolled as a special student with the junior class in 1891. Although ineligible for a degree, he entered academic life with characteristic enthusiasm. In addition, his gay, gregarious nature brought him many friends, and he immediately became lost in the dizzy whirl of the Ivy Club, the Glee Club, and the Dramatic Association. From a literary standpoint, "he had the unique distinction of serving as an editor for three major student publications: the *Nassau Literary Magazine,* the *Tiger,* and the *Bric-a-Brac.*"[11] Although most of his under-

graduate writing consists of campus ephemera, his prose pieces
show a quickening awareness of style and a growth in narrative
skill. "The Better Man," his prize story for the literary magazine,
is a realistic sketch which prefigures much of his writing during
the middle years.

In many ways Princeton provided a liberal education for the
provincial Midwesterner. Although he remarked much later to
a friend that "the Ivy prestige is as ridiculous a thing as comes
under my observation,"[12] he looked back with increasing fond-
ness upon his Princeton days; and he remained a loyal alumnus.
As a member of an informal literary club known as the Coffee
House, he engaged in many heated discussions of all the standard
eighteenth-century authors (of whom he was especially fond),
as well as in more controversial debates over such "modern"
figures as George Meredith, William Dean Howells, Rudyard
Kipling, and Henry James. Booth's classwork brought him
unsuspected rewards in such diverse areas as science and ethics;
his extracurricular activities proved of inestimable worth in
his later forays into both publishing and the theater. In fact,
Woodress labels Princeton "the pivotal experience of his youth."

## CHAPTER 2

# The Writer on Trial

TARKINGTON returned to Indianapolis from college with neither a profession nor a job. He did have an ambition— to become a writer; but, as he later confessed, "there was a vast difference between wanting to write and succeeding at it." The approved method, of course, was to establish oneself in an accepted vocation and then to take up writing as a tangential avocation as Booth's fellow Hoosiers had done or were doing: Edward Eggleston had been a Methodist circuit-rider, Lew Wallace had combined military and legal careers with his writing, and James Whitcomb Riley was a veteran lecturer as well as a grass-roots poet.

## I  The Socio-economic Climate

Considering the general plight of the artist in a down-to-earth, pragmatic America, Tarkington was singularly blessed. As the result of the generosity of indulgent parents and the legacy from his uncle, the young man was able to pursue for nearly six years at home his avowed career as writer. According to his own report, Tarkington netted exactly twenty-two dollars and fifty cents during this period; but no evidence exists that his parents ever questioned his course of action. Instead, they shared with him their growing family fortune, taking him on extended summer vacation trips and encouraging a busy social calendar.

For the aspiring author, however, the years from mid-1893 to late 1899 were marked by failures and frustrations. Manuscripts for short stories were sent and returned with unbroken regularity, ambitious novels refused to be completed, and

promising plays met only local acceptance. To all outward
appearances, Tarkington was as complete a failure as one could
imagine, and the whole period was a waste of time. In reality,
these years of apprenticeship proved of inestimable value to
the young writer. Not only did he extend his knowledge of
persons and places amid a variety of circumstances, but he
learned also the discipline of work. Like Hawthorne in this
respect, Tarkington practiced his craft diligently to make each
piece the very best he could produce. As in no other period of
a work-filled career, during these post-Princeton years Tarkington advanced far in the transformation of his talent into art.

It must be admitted that at no time, now or later, did Tarkington know the desolation of poverty or the degradation of need,
nor do any of his works deal with characters in dire straits.
In a Dreiserian way, Tarkington had little contact with life
"on the other side of the tracks"; hence, he avoided in his fiction
both naked squalor and raw violence. In all likelihood, even
had he been subjected personally to such aspects of life, his
inbred sense of decorum would have denied the suitability of
such experience for literature.

Paradoxically, Tarkington suffered most from his critics because of this very absence of suffering. Indeed, one of his
gravest blunders was his choice of birthplace, parents, and
upbringing. Later, of course, life dealt differently with him:
he teetered on the brink of alcoholism, he underwent an igno-
minious divorce, he buried his only child, he fought a long
campaign with blindness. According to his own tenets, such
desolating experiences were ample preparation for him to deal
with "real life."

As a matter of record, some aspects of the shifting sociocultural scene in the closing years of the nineteenth century
find only dim reflections in the writings of Tarkington. The
genteel respectability of his home background and private-school
experiences precluded intimacy with the appalling labor conditions of his formative years. In 1886, the violence of the brutal
Anarchist riot at Haymarket Square erupted in nearby Chicago
when Tarkington was an impressionable seventeen; half a state
away, in 1894 a ragtag Coxey's Army of the unemployed assembled at Massillon, Ohio, for its march on Washington, D.C.,

while Tarkington was launching his struggle for publication. Even John Hay's "splendid little war" four years later left no scars upon a Tarkington absorbed in reworking his "Indiana novel."

As a result, the dramatic record of the "robber barons," the "revolt of the proletriat," and the journal of the militarists are not found in Booth Tarkington's books. His developmental period, still ruled by the giants of a declining age, was predominantly one of artistic refinement and polite restraint. All of his peers were respected "gentlemen," and only a few among them would even have acknowledged the literary "upstarts" who were rising against them. Still fewer knew then that their Brahmin world was fated to become the legacy of the Bohemians. For, as J. Isaacs has stated in *An Assessment of Twentieth Century Literature,* "The twentieth century was being dovetailed into the nineteenth, and striding across the join was the new figure who was to own the new century—the Common Man."[1] Unlike a Jack London or a Theodore Dreiser, Tarkington was not a "common man" in the popular sense of the phrase—and none knew it better than he. But, as many have learned to their sorrow, no man can be every man; and Tarkington early resolved that he would do his best at appraising his talents, at assessing his resources, and proceed therefrom. That he made errors in his estimates in certain areas, none will dispute; that he miscalculated in certain judgments, most will agree. On the other side of the ledger, although he left untried several aspects of Americana which since have swollen in significance, perhaps he compensated by mastery over his chosen areas.

Early in his career as a critic, Bernard DeVoto made the statement that "novelists are among the least observant of human beings; they are practically impermeable by what goes on around them except as it can come through channels of personal reference."[2] Certainly this statement is true of Booth Tarkington. As mentioned earlier, much of national and international import seemingly passed by him as he explored his own resources. And certainly his most trenchant works are those in which he "came home to Indiana." In novel after novel he exhibited keen observation, acute hearing, and sensitive perceptions; he also absorbed the historical heritage that was his through wide reading, frequent chats with folk of any age or race, and a voluminous correspondence. Henry Steele Commager once commented, "If you want to know what houses looked like, outside and inside; how men and women dressed; how they spoke; how they behaved; you can go to Tarkington. He had an eye for detail."[3]

In much the same vein, Robert Coates Holliday remarked in an early critical essay, "Extraordinary among Mr. Tarkington's books for its length of years, *The Magnificent Ambersons* is extraordinary in American literature as a reference volume. It bridges the gulf in memory between an obsolete world and today.... The rise, the flowering, the decay of a whole epoch in American civilization is mirrored in this chronicle of the splendor of the Ambersons which lasted throughout all the years that saw their Midland town spread and darken into a city."[4] To fellow-Hoosier Meredith Nicholson as well, it was apparent that, "just as Eggleston and Riley left records of their respective generations, so Mr. Tarkington, arriving opportunely to preserve unbroken the apostolic succession, depicts his own day with the effect of contributing a third panel in a series of historical paintings."[5]

## II   *The Rejection of Naturalism*

Because of Tarkington's penchant for verisimilitude, we must not infer that he should be identified with the Naturalist school of fiction in subject matter or with its emphasis upon reportorial style. At every period in Tarkington's career he was by no means immune to literary influences from a variety of sources, but Naturalism was not one of them. He decided early upon an artistic code based upon imaginative truth rather than upon factual report. As J. Donald Adams explains in *The Shape of Books to Come*, to the Naturalistic novelist "imagination has no longer a place.... You simply take the life study of a person or a group of persons, whose actions you faithfully depict. The work becomes a report, nothing more; it has but the merit of exact observation, of more or less profound penetration and analysis, of the logical connection of facts." Naturalism implies that "you start from the point that nature (both human and extra-human) is sufficient, that you must accept it as it is, without modification or pruning; it is grand enough, beautiful enough, to supply its own beginning, its middle, and its end."[6]

Such a dictum held small appeal for Tarkington; to him, it ignored those basic artistic principles of selection and arrangement which he considered fundamental in both literature and pictorial art. To his mind, the creed of Naturalism allowed nothing for that elusive alchemy of the artist whereby the thing observed is not merely reproduced by a clever reporter but interpreted by peculiar genius in such a way as to reveal its inner significance, as well as its external appearance. In much the same way, Tarkington rejected the element of determinism which pervaded the Naturalistic code. Whereas he was not a denominationalist, he was a profoundly spiritual man. His parents, loyal Presbyterians who attended services regularly, compelled their young son to sit through "interminable sermons" with them. "The boredom of those painful Sundays," Tarkington recalled much later, "has remained with me all my life." One result, of course, was that he was never in his adult years a regular churchgoer. But another was that he nurtured that somewhat amorphous Protestantism which so often develops alongside "middle-class respectability."

Within this creed (perhaps better termed "attitude") lie most of those social principles which are usually identified as "American ideals." Based largely upon the premise of "the brotherhood of man under the fatherhood of God," these principles reflect the religious idealism in America which has led to rugged Jacksonian democracy, to Transcendental humanitarianism, and to belligerent Whitmanian equalitarianism. To Tarkington, it meant a deep-rooted conviction that America held within itself a complex of Christian tenets by which it had risen to high status and to which it had to adhere if it were to maintain that position.

One factor within this complex was faith in a Higher Power. By the turn of the nineteenth century, Tarkington was appalled by the mounting skepticism engendered by the "New Mechanism," as Lewis Mumford labeled it in "A Modern Synthesis." Although bolstered by such stalwarts as Sir Charles Lyell, Charles Darwin, and Herbert Spencer, such a mechanistic philosophy

struck the conservative novelist as the virtual reduction of man
to a machine and life to an equation. Branding the movement
in *The Midlander* (1924) as "a newer and more gorgeous
materialism," Tarkington declared that "it began to breed, among
other things, a new critic [of religion] who attacked every faith,
and offered, instead of mysteries, full knowledge of all creation
as merely a bit of easily comprehended mechanics."[7]

To the proponents of the New Mechanism, to the practitioners
of the "eat, drink, and be merry" hedonism so prevalent in the
1920's, to the nihilists of the Hemingway coterie, he posed the
question: What have you to offer in response to the Whence,
the Why, and the Whither of Existence? To the inheritor of the
Christian tradition, passed down from his Methodist grandfather
and Presbyterian parents, there was no reply but faith in some
divinity whom one might as well call God. "I couldn't find
the answers by what we sometimes call philosophizing,"[8] Tarkington admitted; neither could he embrace the creed of any
denomination. Tarkington's solution to the dilemma was simple—
hold firm to the elemental faith of the child. Science leads only
from the explanation of one mystery to the revelation of another;
logic leads only from the explication of one enigma to the
fabrication of another. Well aware of sectarian dissension and
metaphysical controversy, Tarkington withdrew at an early age
into his own refuge of quiet faith.

Central to this faith is Tarkington's belief in a continuum
of being. Like many another, Tarkington sought some reassuring
answer to the ultimate question, that of death. As he relates
his search in the preface to an intriguing volume of short stories,
Tarkington found confirmation to his trust in the continuity
of life in the words of a homely ditch-digger who had lost his
son three years earlier: "Him and me, we're all the same as
mud and moon and sun and stars; always the same, always
will be."[9] As narrator Tarkington pondered the remark, it was
evident that the old man "had the feeling that the universe
was immortal.... Therefore every part of it was immortal
and he and his dead son were immortal; there was no death,
there was only change."[10] In the great cosmic sweep of man
and matter, nothing is lost; all serve one end, then another, in
an unbroken cycle of perpetual re-creation. Such a philosophy,

coupled with supreme confidence in a benevolent deity, explains to a great extent Tarkington's optimistic temper and resilient nature.

There remains a related aspect which Tarkington deemed important: not only did the Naturalists recognize a mechanistic universe governed by immutable natural forces, but they likewise regarded man as just another manifestation of nature governed largely by forces beyond his control. These forces thus become the determinant factors in life—among them the biological determinism of Charles Darwin, the sociological determinism of Herbert Spencer, the economic determinism of Karl Marx, and the psychological determinism of Sigmund Freud. They denied that the great American Dream held before every man the freedom of choice that led him into his vocation, his religion, his political party, and even his social class. Thus there remains, especially among Tarkington's more thoughtful works, a frequent reminder that "life is pretty much what you make it," and only when one misleads or is misled does one run into the complications that make fiction.

Finding Naturalism to be inimical to his artistic temperament, as well as to his religious ideals, Tarkington numbered himself among the high majority of the "bourgeois gentility" of his time to whom Naturalism in literature meant, as Maxwell Geismar indicates, "novels of low-life, of crime, drink, and vice, or the debased animal instincts in man."[11] Regardless of the original intentions of proponents of Naturalism to apply the methods of modern science to the province of the arts, and in other areas to utilize such information for the enhancement of literature and esthetics, the popular mind associated it with the extremes of radicalism.

Yet Tarkington would have been in complete sympathy with Irwin Edman, who commented in 1929 in an essay called "Patterns for the Free": "The revolts against tradition have often been explained away as the mere exhibitionism of literary eccentrics or writers perversely weary of beautiful classic molds. On the contrary, the desire for change at this time is far more plausibly explained by the rise of mechanical science, the spread of industry, and the sophistication of psychology, than by any merely personal foible of an abstract *litterateur*."[12] Here, as in other places as well, Tarkington was by no means a mere advocate of the status quo. One of his most provocative works is entitled *The World Does Move*, and his progressivism in various guises should be noted. As already mentioned, Tarkington encouraged change toward an ultimate better world as a normal concomitant of progress; what he deplored was undisciplined rebellion. Only too often, he observed, "intelligent revolt... becomes in time indiscriminate, because continued rebellion always loses discrimination."[13] That is, what he labeled the "prettifying and too-sweet sweetness and sentimentality" of mid-Victorian literature needed the salutary effects of artistic and critical revolt; but such a revolt must be conducted within the bounds of decorum and restraint. Continental Naturalism, he felt, transgressed the limits of propriety and sought acclaim on the ground of shock appeal rather than artistic merit.

Minor conflicts of Tarkington with Naturalism are discussed later in this study, but the foregoing points are the major reasons Tarkington felt at variance with it. Posterity, of course, has sided rather solidly in favor of the impact of Naturalism upon contemporary American letters, and this attitude is one important reason for the comparative neglect today of Tarkington's work. As recently as 1960, Willard Thorp commented in *American Writing in the Twentieth Century*: "For more than fifty years there has been a persistent bias towards naturalism in American thought as well as in the novel. This bias has become deeply ingrained in the American mind. Events and ideas decade by decade have combined to strengthen it."[14] Thorp demonstrates, however, that Naturalism is not now what it was in 1900. Today, he asserts, "modern naturalism has a cheerful tone because it finds much good within actual existence...; likewise, contemporary literary naturalists are much less concerned with heredity than were the followers of Zola who thought the theory of atavistic reversion could explain why man behaved in such nasty ways." Perhaps most important in its relation to Tarkington is Thorp's conclusion that "Modern philosophical naturalism avoids bleak determinism. It permits man a large measure of free will operative in his own life and in the society in which he lives."[15]

We do not intend to renew the "war of the critics" which

has flared sporadically across some three-quarters of a century between the rival camps of the Realists and the Naturalists. After analyzing the issue on such bases as relative degrees of emphasis on various subjects; the relative amount of attention on theme, plot, or characterization; and the relative impacts of central forces like money, sex, or prestige, we are tempted to agree with Philip Rahv that "... there are no hard and fast rules that can be used to distinguish the naturalist method from the methods of realism generally."[16] In the case of Tarkington, the issue was more a matter of selection and rejection rather than one of adaptation or acceptance, so far as Naturalism was concerned. For varying reasons, he was more interested in the Realism of Howells, the veritism of Garland, and the regionalism of Mark Twain.

### III  *The Lures of the Regional*

During the period of Tarkington's apprenticeship, his consuming interest was publication. With a steady barrage of stories, one-act plays, and even cartoons, he invaded editorial offices of every type. In 1900 he confessed, "I was for five years, and more, one of the rejected—as continuously and successively, I suppose, as anyone who ever wrote."[17] During this period, he later joked, he sent countless manuscripts to editors in New York which came back so promptly that they seemed to have been intercepted in Philadelphia. But rejection taught him much of practical value. Perhaps of most immediate importance, it taught him to study the reading tastes of the time and then to match them.

Eventually, Tarkington discovered the cardinal principle governing popular literary taste: all the world loves a romance. This statement Tarkington himself would abjure soon after his literary arrival, but at the turn of the century it seemed to him to offer the surest promise of recognition—publication, that is. Although fraught with insidious dangers, although certain to rouse the condemnation of critics like Howells, although fated with Tarkington to adulterate nearly every endeavor, romance held for him the assurance of swift and wide approval from the many readers who preferred it and from the editors who catered to such readers. Tarkington then was young, he was ambitious, he was eager; and, we might also add, he was himself romantic.

As we noted earlier, he was not alone in this last respect. Although not so labeled in American literature texts, from the standpoint of general reading tastes, his was truly "a romantic age." In a 1929 *Saturday Review of Literature* article entitled "Let Us Confound Them," Tarkington wrote of the widespread reader resentment in the late nineteenth century toward the "dissection and analysis, then called realism," of the emergent Naturalist school. "What the opposition principally wanted and championed, instead of realism, was romance," Tarkington explained. "Don't talk to us about everyday life and everyday people. Don't talk to us about ourselves and our humdrum lives. We know too much about all that already, without being told. . . . Don't write about commonplaces; write of the unusual or the heroic or the ideal. Entertain us and lift us out of ourselves."[18] The obvious problem for an author anxious to meet popular fancy was to contrive a tale pleasantly remote in either time or place, or preferably both, which would contain within it all the color, the pageantry, the gusto so lacking in the ordinary round of life. The equally obvious solution was that genre in imaginative prose known most politely as "the historical romance."

Every survey of the novel of this period reveals the upsurge of the historical romance. In an informal report published in the "Trade Winds" column of the *Saturday Review*, Bennett Cerf listed the "most popular" novels of that time on the basis of library demand: beginning with 1897, *Quo Vadis* by Henry Sienkiewicz; 1898, *Hugh Wynne* by S. Weir Mitchell; 1899, *Richard Carvel* by Winston Churchill; 1900, *To Have and to Hold* by Mary Johnson; 1901, *Graustark* by George Barr McCutcheon; and 1902, *The Virginian* by Owen Wister. A similar list, supplemented by such Continental favorites as Anthony Hope, Rudyard Kipling, and Marie Corelli, may be found in Frank Luther Mott's study, *Golden Multitudes: The Story of Best Sellers in the United States*. (In this latter work, by the way, Tarkington's best sellers are listed: *The Gentleman from Indiana*, 1899; *Penrod*, 1914; *The Turmoil*, 1915; and *Seventeen*, 1916.)

For Tarkington, fresh from Princeton when the movement was just gathering momentum, the vogue was a happy coincidence; for historical romance was perhaps the most congenial area for the aspiring novelist. In his childhood, he had been enthralled by pages from the past; later, in Tarkington's experimental years, as Walter Schmauch reports, "the eighteenth-century writers, particularly the French School of Balzac, Daudet, and Dumas, were the patterns for Tarkington's earlier works."[19] To the purist, the interbreeding of fact and fancy to produce historical romance results in a bastardized offspring which is neither good history nor good fiction. To the young Tarkington, such a combination seemed a pleasant way to surmount an unpleasant situation; he liked both history and literature; he knew others enjoyed the combination; he found it difficult to break into print; therefore, he would write historical romances.

For his own good as a maturing novelist, Tarkington probably devoted too much of his apprenticeship to various forays into romance. Proceeding from college-period pieces for an abortive literary magazine, to summertime costume playlets for local production, to unproduced Broadway offerings, he labored in this vein for nearly a decade. Several fragments of more solid promise emerged during these years, but they never achieved coherent completion. We sense his need for critical direction from an experienced hand at this stage, but the only literary counsel he received was from James Whitcomb Riley. Hauté, hoping to help her inept brother, sent the manuscript of a delightful eighteenth-century pastiche called "Mr. Brooks" to the Hoosier poet (and family friend) for critical reactions. They were immediate—and violent. Riley, who had no patience with historical fiction, wholly mistook the artificial style and fired back the manuscript with a comment on the final sheet to the effect that the tale was "pure Goldsmith," that Tarkington's archaisms were "affectations," and that he "should know better."[20]

More amused than dismayed by this episode, Tarkington revived an earlier story—a costume romance—which had been inspired by one of his own pen-and-ink sketches. Sent to a monthly magazine, it was shipped right back; but the rejection was an error: "The editor who turned down *Monsieur Beaucaire* lost an opportunity to buy a manuscript that quickly reached the best-seller lists after McClure published it, and it thereafter continued to prosper. Eventually it provided Richard Mansfield and Lewis Waller with plays, British and American companies with operettas, Rudolph Valentino and Bob Hope with movies, at least eight anthologists with selections, and countless readers with a pleasant story that never has been out of print."[21]

Although the time came when Tarkington himself thought lightly of such "trifles," F. L. Pattee attests that "by more than one critic *Monsieur Beaucaire* has been rated as one of the most brilliant short stories of its period."[22] Not only is it a well-constructed story, but it remains a charming evocation of eighteenth-century England during the reign of Beau Nash. The adventures of the Duke of Orleans, as he exposes the snobbery and duplicity of the period while tarrying at Bath, make truly "a little literary cameo," as Damon Runyon described it forty years later in the Indianapolis *Star*.

Upon a number of occasions, Tarkington capitalized upon this happy combination of his own felicity in creating historical romances and the avidity of the public in demanding them; but, at the same time, he had no illusions as to their true literary nature. Even while *Monsieur Beaucaire* was in press following its serialization, Tarkington sent McClure an earlier experimental novelette entitled *Cherry*. This quite forgotten gem, which Joseph Collins ranks as "one of Tarkington's most artistic tales," is a delicious burlesque upon the historical romance in general, and upon Winston Churchill's *Richard Carvel* in particular. Set vaguely on the campus of eighteenth-century Princeton, *Cherry* introduces a prissy young collegian named Sudgeberry, who proceeds to display himself as an impossible prude. The dual elements of satire, one on the historical novel *per se* and one on priggish human nature, impose a problem on interpretation with which few have chosen to cope. Ever the optimist, Tarkington wrote shortly after its delayed appearance between boards that "*Cherry* will get by, if taken on the grounds of its intention—but if you read it as a *story,* it's all off!" It did not "get by." Years later when he looked back upon its quiet death, he realized that "No one ever saw what I was up to!"[23]

Competent though Tarkington became in the field of historical romance, his initial success was in a somewhat different area. In the autumn of 1893, his first year out of college, he began *The Gentleman from Indiana.* Some forty thousand words were written within a few months, then "it wouldn't budge." After no amount of tinkering seemed to avail, Tarkington laid aside the unfinished manuscript and returned to his short stories and plays. Over the next five years, however, he came back to the novel with renewed insight and enthusiasm, completing the work in early 1898. In several respects, it provides an interesting study in contrasts to his historical romances.

From his birth in 1869, Tarkington had grown up during the era of what is now labeled "the local color movement," which burgeoned in the 1870's and 1880's and then blossomed into regionalism in the new century. As F. O. Matthiessen points out, "Fiction was everywhere seeking new materials to exploit; and local areas of Europe, as well as the United States, were ready to supply them in the richest abundance."[24] In America, impelled in part by the infection of frontier humor like that of Sut Lovingood and Simon Suggs, the growth of sectional legends like those of Davy Crockett and Mike Fink, and the influence of such comic journalists as Artemus Ward and Mark Twain, the local-color movement spread over the entire nation.

In the Midlands of Indiana, this regionalism was identified with the Hoosier School, a loose aggregate of authors in the state who popularized both historical romance and local-color literature. Much of the writing in the latter category sprang from provincial pride, and Tarkington would be the first to admit that *The Gentleman from Indiana* "was inspired by a genuine desire to extol the virtue of his native state."[25] As a novel, it also conforms admirably to the requisites listed by Frederick Lewis Allen for a best-seller in 1899. On the basis of a study Allen made from *Publisher's Weekly* reports, he concluded, "Even the most cautious scholar ... might see ... signs of a mingling of two popular predilections: one for picturesque romance, preferably historical; the other, for homely sentiment, rural simplicity and virtue, and homely humor."[26] It would be difficult to find more apt terms than these to describe the dominant qualities of *The Gentleman from Indiana.* It gained

its approval from "the manly virtue" of the hero and "the
feminine purity" of the heroine, it is laden indeed with "homely
sentiment," and it overflows with "the beautiful people" of
its Hoosier heartland.

No better proof of Tarkington's skill in sounding public
taste can be adduced than the emergence of the young author
at the turn of the century, equipped with publishable items
in both varieties of the best-seller, though Tarkington himself
was beginning to despair of success. It was his sister, Hauté,
who finally opened the editorial door. Unknown to her brother,
she carried in person the manuscript of *Monsieur Beaucaire* to
the office of publisher S. S. McClure in New York and requested
his examination of the work. Surfeited at the moment with
derring-do tales, McClure was just about to dismiss his visitor
when she mentioned another work, "a Hoosier story." Scenting in
the Indiana novel a promising regional romance, McClure asked
Hauté to have Tarkington forward *The Gentleman from Indiana*
to him. Thrilled by his sister's achievement but still skeptical of
the outcome, Tarkington mailed his bulky manuscript to McClure.
Two weeks passed; then came a letter from a reader for *Mc-
Clure's Magazine*. Without prologue it began: "Mr. McClure has
given me your manuscript, *The Gentleman from Indiana,* to read.
You are a novelist." The letter was signed: "Hamlin Garland."[27]

## CHAPTER 3

# The Age of Romance

T HE affirmation from Hamlin Garland provided a great lift to Tarkington's morale. Four decades later, in a posthumous tribute to his fellow novelist, Tarkington recalled the thrill of the declaration: "You are a novelist." "I couldn't imagine anybody's saying such a thing," he wrote, "and last of all could I have believed that an accredited novelist would ever say it; but after I came to know Hamlin Garland I found that nothing was more typical of him than his stopping work to write such a letter to a groping, unknown youth dismally mystified about himself and the art of writing."[1]

Actually, these two authors were closer to their literary ideologies than either of them suspected in that terminal year of the nineteenth century. In *Crumbling Idols,* published some five years earlier in 1895, Garland had described a code of literary principles under the generic label "veritism" to which Tarkington gladly would have subscribed. "Art is an individual thing," Garland declared, "the question of one man facing certain facts and telling his individual relations to them. His first care must be to present his own concept. This is, I believe, the essence of veritism. Write of those things of which you know most, and for which you care most. By so doing you will be true to yourself, true to your locality, and true to your time."[2] The native Hoosier writing of his own state and the native resident writing of his own Indianapolis conform neatly to Garland's dicta. Indeed, the practical Mr. Tarkington later admitted, "I had no real success until I struck Indiana subjects."

I   *The Gentleman from Indiana*

In the next mail after the note from Hamlin Garland, a
letter arrived from S. S. McClure, editor of *McClure's Monthly
Magazine*, which called for immediate action. "We accept your
manuscript to be published in book form," wrote the editor in
mid-January of 1899, "and we are considering it for serial
publication in the magazine, though for this purpose you
would have to cut it almost in half. If the idea interests you,
perhaps you'd better come to New York as soon as you can."[3]
After a hectic weekend, Tarkington boarded the train on Monday
in Indianapolis as an unknown scribbler who had devoted nearly
six years to his traditional "literary apprenticeship." Two days
later, on Wednesday, February 1, 1899, he "entered with
trepidation" the New York office of the McClure publishing
company and a writing career of almost unbroken achievement
that persisted to his death in 1946. Barton Currie, for many
years a close associate of Tarkington both as editor and friend,
remarked shortly after Tarkington's death: "To the best of my
recollection, supported by an examination of the records, there
was no period longer than six months within a span of forty-
eight years when Tarkington failed to produce."[4]

McClure forecast that morning the Tarkington fortune with
remarkable accuracy. Shortly after introductions were over,
Tarkington reported in a prompt letter to his "honored Parents
and Sister" that the editor had turned to him and said: "Yes;
it's decided . . . [*The Gentleman from Indiana* is] to go in the
magazine. You may not think it's remarkable that you've written
a book that makes you the only man we'll publish along with
Kipling as a serialist—but we are turning down a serial by
Anthony Hope of *Prisoner of Zenda* fame to put in this of
yours. We are going to push you and make you known everywhere—you are to be the greatest of the new generation, and
we'll help you to be."[5] Moments later, when Ida Tarbell (a
Lincoln enthusiast and a pioneer Muckraker) came into his
office, McClure introduced an abashed Tarkington by proclaim-
ing, "Miss Tarbell, this is to be the most famous young man
in America." Small wonder the modest Hoosier confessed, "I felt
like a large gray ass—and looked it!"[6]

The next few weeks in New York assumed an aura of fantasy which might well have swept an aspiring writer quite off his literary feet. It was probably fortunate for his ego that serial publication of *The Gentleman from Indiana* necessitated the painful excision of forty thousand words from a work which already had been shaped and trimmed over many months. Some two weeks after his arrival in the city, he wrote his parents, "I have sweat over the serial a lot"; but he was only beginning. An indication of the labor that went into the magazine version of the novel is the fact that Tarkington was held in the city by his publishers from February until early May.

At the same time, Tarkington's social life was far from neglected. True to his word, McClure spared no effort at "pushing and helping" to make his young author known. Soon after meeting the editorial staff at *McClure's,* Tarkington began a busy series of luncheons, dinners, and weekends with persons of literary prominence—men ranging from Rudyard Kipling to Paul Leicester Ford to Ernest Thompson Seton. Already a member of the Princeton Club, Tarkington was issued guest cards to the Century Club and to the Players Club. Thus, early in his career he began to form a circle of friendships among the genteel *literati* of that time which would grow larger and stronger throughout his life.

It is abundantly clear that Tarkington acquitted himself well during these months with McClure. Not only did he compress his novel successfully into the required number of monthly installments, each of the proper length, but he also developed the knack of tying together these segments by means of ingenious subclimaxes and trim transitions. Tarkington made such an impression on McClure that, before he had been in the city two weeks, Tarkington wrote his family that the editor had invited him "to go abroad with them and stay the summer at a house they have in Besenval, southern France—Alps in fall." By way of inducement, McClure "said he'll give me $200 more for the serial if I'd come."[7] Although the invitation was refused, McClure shortly thereafter hinted that he might find a position for Tarkington with a new publishing venture he was considering. With surprising independence for one so new in the profession, Tarkington also rejected this proffer. "I wouldn't take it if I could," he told his parents; "...it would be an end to writing and the Golden Goose would lay no more eggs."[8]

The May issue of *McClure's Magazine* preceded Tarkington's return to Indianapolis just long enough for him to find the novel the topic of much discussion. He also found that "no longer was Judge Tarkington accused of supporting in idleness a writer-son whose stories no editor wanted."[9] As a matter of record, Tarkington received only six hundred dollars from McClure for the serial rights to publish *The Gentleman from Indiana*; but, when the novel appeared in book form in late autumn, it became an immediate best-seller which launched him into fame.

The immediate success of Tarkington's first publication was not the product of chance. As he wrote his mother, he was a self-taught critic who had "studied his profession and the ways of getting ahead in it very hard." In brief, he now felt some competence in his literary craftsmanship—some confidence in his appraisal of the literary market. In addition, he had been most fortunate to encounter a sympathetic novelist like Hamlin Garland as the reader of his manuscript for *McClure's Magazine*. No doubt, Garland in part approved of *The Gentleman from Indiana* because it depicted the society of his native Midwest as he liked to remember it; even more so, he realized that it presented American life as the vast citizenry would like to conceive it.

With engaging freshness, Tarkington had reversed the usual pattern of having a provincial hero strike out for the big city of the East to make his fortune. Instead, he told the story of John Harkless, a stalwart young man from the East, who arrives in Plattville, Indiana, to revive a run-down weekly newspaper. Harkless transforms the *Herald* into an effective weapon to fight for justice, honor, and decency against a lawless mob of "Whitecaps," who add no little to the excitement. In addition, of course, Tarkington managed a romantic interest with considerable skill. Helen Sherwood, admittedly an idealized character, has a winsomeness and charm that still delight. In fact, her combination of cool independence and feminine helplessness set a model which Tarkington often used in subsequent novels.

John Harkless, the indomitable editor, was in part an extension of John Cleve Green, Tarkington's closest friend at Princeton, who died suddenly in 1897. Two years later Tarkington dedicated to him *The Gentleman from Indiana* as a memorial to their friendship. In addition, whenever the young Harkless recalls his college days or yearns for greater journalistic recognition, Tarkington is drawing from his own recent past. Indeed, as Woodress affirms, "Although it is sentimentally romantic, the novel is overlaid with a realistic patina deriving from the author's memories."[10] As a result, the work contains authentic local color which enriches many a page with Hoosier dialect and Midwestern settings.

In all probability, the real popularity of *The Gentleman from Indiana* sprang from "the manly virtues of the hero and the feminine charm of the heroine." Its readers encountered no difficulty in identifying themselves most pleasantly with such idealized characters; and, when their vicarious experiences turned out satisfactorily, they too were satisfied. A later Tarkington held such novelistic technique in low critical esteem; for, instead of inviting the reader to identify himself with a chief character, the mature Tarkington declared that the truly worthwhile novel "paints—reveals—and keeps to the *detached* view of the sheer artist. It can live with the reader only by virtue of its insight and its craftsmanship in revelation—in other words, by the distinction of its writing. Therefore its perceptive readers must be relatively few."[11] (It is interesting to note that Tarkington recognized Henry James to be the peerless practitioner of this kind of writing, for Tarkington has been categorized in recent years with the "faded gentility" of the Jamesian school.)

Tarkington would be the first to confess that *The Gentleman from Indiana* was designed in part as a defense of his native state. He also would maintain that native pride, artistically controlled, is valid motivation for a national literature. Indeed, to the Hoosier novelist there was nothing mawkish about regional pride. In 1902, reacting to the charges of sentimentality in the novel, he wrote a spirited defense of the Ohio Valley and its people. These Midlanders, he asserted, "are pleasant people to know; easy-going, yet not happy-go-lucky; possessing energy without rush, and gayety without extravagance." With easy humor and frequent anecdote he described their "way of being hospitable without exertion," their lack of snobbishness, their "large quantity of small gossip," but their relative freedom from "real scandal." Although he admits that "life is exceedingly dull at times," we sense throughout his essay on "The Middle West" an abiding love for the Midland society which dominates his better works.

For several reasons, then, *The Gentleman from Indiana* was a popular novel. It made the "best-seller" list for 1899 in Mott's *Golden Multitudes* and also the monthly best-seller lists twice in 1900. Subsequently, it has run through numerous domestic and foreign editions; it was adapted for a motion picture; and it has been excerpted frequently for anthologies. For the new novelist, it proved a veritable bonanza; the income from the novel supplemented his uncle's modest legacy, and Tarkington enjoyed a handsome income that seldom languished thereafter.

## II  *Tarkington and William Dean Howells*

On November 18, 1899, novelist-critic William Dean Howells visited Indianapolis. As a result of shrewd politicking on the part of Mrs. Ovid Jameson, née Hauté Tarkington, his escort that day was Booth Tarkington. Actually, this meeting was their second one; five years earlier a self-conscious baritone from the Men's Glee Club of Princeton had quavered through an unaccompanied solo before Howells at the Lantern Club in New York City. After Howells declared he had forgotten the incident, the two men shared a pleasant afternoon in easy conversation. Perhaps Tarkington regarded the elder novelist with too much awe, for it is evident that he did not engage Howells in serious matters of authorship upon this occasion. Later that evening, Howells told an interviewer that he had read *The Gentleman from Indiana* "with pleasure"; and he added that "Mr. Tarkington was an author of great promise." But such praise for a man he barely knew and for a novel which he later disparaged for its "romanticism" suggests that the visitor spoke more from graciousness than from conviction.

En route to the lecture hall after dinner, Howells did give his disciple a few words of advice. In particular, he warned,

"Beware the critics. You'll find they can still hurt you long after their power to please you is gone!"[12] As the author of a long list of works which already were beginning to lose their original charm—and hence the enthusiasm of critics—Howells knew whereof he spoke. As an author, Tarkington learned early enough that he "was to follow one of those callings that of their very nature bring not one but a horde of critics, seemingly out of nowhere, to beset the path indignantly."[13] Although rarely assaulted by the "mosquito-minded," as he termed them, his opinion of professional critics in general was by no means flattering. More often than not, it seemed to him, such persons devoted more space to airing their own opinions than to the subjects at hand. "Such pompous criticism," he commented, "is no more . . . than the autobiography of critics, revealing their taste and education, each bit of it wearing forty masks and setting up to be the whole academy."[14]

Despite Tarkington's own university background, he apparently attributed little credit to academic criticism as well. Writing within the security of private correspondence, he confided to his college classmate Julian Green that "Professors don't know about writing. 'Literature' for them is a museum: they're curators and look after the dusting of classic curios . . . and when they try to *make* opinions . . . they just gesture with their dust-rag."[15] Like Sinclair Lewis, he especially resented the reluctance with which the academic critic approached current literary works. Near the end of his own career, Tarkington lamented that "The man purely of letters will have his artists dead (or very foreign) before he so honors them as to chop them up into little laws for the living." After all, he queried in the same article, "Is a man's quality to be judged by all his work, or by his best, or by his worst? There's no law on the question—we may choose which course we'll take, and the one we choose depends, with most of us, merely upon our own dispositions and congenialities."[16]

If scholarly critics insisted upon maintaining a "pompous" attitude, if they persisted in displaying their snobbish sophistication, if they were determined to transform living letters into problems of casuistry, he would be content to rest his case with the reading public who enjoyed his books. "Only

the people can bestow the laurel" was his favorite way of
expressing this conviction. In his tribute to William Dean
Howells upon the death of his mentor, Tarkington asserted,
"In the long run, the people recommend a work of art to the
pompous critic; they sometimes take his recommendation temporarily; but for permanent use it is he who takes theirs, yet remains
unaware that his pomposity is thus, after all, a meekness."[17]

The foregoing pronouncements, of course, came long after
the lecture that night in the Plymouth Church. An urbane
Howells, completely at ease, spoke on "Novels and Novel-
Writing." In typical form, he launched into a broadside attack
upon the historical romance, climaxing his denunciation by
asserting that "Sir Walter Scott continued to be read only by
persons in their nonage." Immediately he sounded his own
campaign cry for Realism: "The truth should always be told.
It may be indecent, but it cannot be vicious. The imagination
can work only with the stub of experience, for experience is
life. The difference between realism and romanticism is that
the realist takes nature as he finds her; the romanticist colors
nature for his own use."[18] Of all the Indiana authors who might
have gained his attention, he reserved his plaudits for but two:
Edward Eggleston (whose *Hoosier Schoolmaster* had appeared
in 1871, the same year Howells had published his first novel)
and James Whitcomb Riley (whom he honored as "the poet of
our common life").

Young Tarkington could well have profited from Howell's
pronouncements about Realism at this formative stage in his
career; in actuality, however, he did not. The man of principle
may have been in full agreement with "the father of American
Realism," but the man of practice pursued a quite different
path throughout his early career. Only in more mature years
did Tarkington develop a firm regard for Howells as the over-
turner of the false gods of decadent Romanticism and as the
founder of an abiding Realism. At the peak of Tarkington's
productive career, Howells was ever the arbiter in matters
literary. When *The Turmoil* was published in 1914, Tarkington
was flattered by both its brisk sale and critical approval; but
he was pleased most of all by the praise of Howells. When the
aging author wrote him warmly about the novel, Tarkington

replied: "Any writer in America would rather have a word from you than from any other man.... It has helped my self-esteem as nothing else could.... You are responsible for whatever good we produce."[19]

Despite their difference in age, a cordial personal regard eventually turned into a warm friendship between the novelists. Tarkington had the privilege, upon the death of the "Dean" in 1920, to write the tribute published by *Harper's*, Howells's old magazine. In this essay Tarkington stressed the artistry of Howells's style, the clarity of his expression, the beauty of his language—qualities that Tarkington appreciated as a fellow craftsman. In full agreement with his own creative ideals, Tarkington could say of Howells: "His first demand, his whole great point for his art, was that fiction should be lifelike; that the picture it made should be truthful. Here was this bookman's real passion, after all—life, not books."[20] To the younger man, Howells held a position of esteem unapproached by any of the new generation soon to sweep the field. Only a short time before Howell's death, Tarkington declared, "When Mr. Howells and the nation agree upon a matter of literature, the rest of us may as well consider that question officially settled."[21] Far from regarding him as "that amiable old maid Howells," as H. L. Mencken tagged him, Tarkington admired his "sweet reasonableness" toward the inexorable shifts in the literary temper, for neither of these men was an iconoclast. Under wholly different circumstances from that of the *Harper's* eulogy, a mellow Tarkington wrote: "Revolutions aren't good for art. Gentle artists die, or vanish; and the other kind tend to become propagandists."[22] With regard to William Dean Howells and others of his ilk, the history of contemporary letters is mute evidence to the truth of this observation.

Once past the lures of romance, Tarkington clearly "considered himself as a perpetuator of the decorous realism that Howells had ably written and critically championed for more than a generation."[23] His own genteel background, coupled with a liberal arts education, imbued him with a strong sympathy for the old-fashioned virtues which Howells personified to him. Like the master before him, Tarkington observed the boundaries of selective realism; despite the impact of mechanistic determinism, he preserved his faith in a spiritualized humanity; despite the pressure of mounting cynicism, he maintained his ebullient optimism.

### III  *The Fruits of Popularity*

Tarkington's final reliance upon "the people" introduces an aspect of his writing career which should be touched upon. In every sense of the word, Tarkington was a "popular" writer. One inevitable result of popularity is money, and Tarkington made a lot of it; in fact, Tarkington died a millionaire. His activities in the novel, the short story, drama, motion pictures, and radio netted him perhaps the top income in American writing history. Personal records in the Tarkington Papers at Princeton indicate that from the six hundred dollars that McClure paid him in 1899 for the serialization of *The Gentleman from Indiana,* Tarkington's rates climbed to sixty thousand dollars for *Mirthful Haven* from the *Saturday Evening Post* in 1930— a depression year. To the esoteric critic, such monetary success is tantamount to artistic failure; to Tarkington, monetary success was the justifiable product of professional craftsmanship.

Another aspect of professionalism soon became evident: in writing, as elsewhere, "nothing succeeds like success." To Tarkington's gratification, he shortly began to realize other returns from the initial success of *The Gentleman from Indiana.* One of these was the immediate interest that publishers exhibited in other words from his pen. *Monsieur Beaucaire,* which had previously gone begging at McClure's, was now snapped up by that magazine, serialized, and then published in book form. While McClure himself was still looking askance at *Cherry,* an off-beat burlesque of period pieces, it was captured by F. H. Sears of *Harper's,* where its publication began for Tarkington a long and profitable alliance with that firm.

In turn, the warm reception given *Monsieur Beaucaire* provided Tarkington with another opening for which he had been searching for several years—the opportunity to produce a work for the stage. Already he had written several one-act plays for local drama clubs and college thespians, as well as a three-act play, *The Prodigals.* This swashbuckling melodrama, laid in the

Trenton, New Jersey, of 1790, was complete with "mistaken identity and heroic self-sacrifice in the best tradition of the costume romance."[24] Its success in 1894 with the Indianapolis Dramatic Club (with the playwright himself assuming the role of the rogue-hero) prompted optimistic friends to see Broadway possibilities for the play. Despite kindly critical comments by Richard Mansfield, the matinee idol of the 1890's, and a cordial invitation to New York by Elizabeth Marbury, a literary agent, Tarkington's first foray into professional theater proved a dismal failure. After repeated rejections in placing *The Prodigals*, Tarkington returned to Indianapolis a disillusioned playwright.

*Beaucaire* as a play (it soon lost the "Monsieur") was another matter—although it too had its trials. Upon its opening "on the road" at the Garrick Theater in Philadelphia on October 7, 1901, the audience was enthusiastic about the production, the reviewers praised the play, and the company looked forward to a long run. When *Beaucaire* reached Broadway, however, fickle tastes had changed. The critics lauded Mansfield the actor, but they were apathetic toward the play itself; the theatergoers followed suit. Back on the road it was a modest success in the States during the "straw-hat circuit," but only after another company took it to England and the Continent, touring for several seasons, did it achieve the notoriety which led to two movie versions.

Once *Beaucaire* was finally launched, Tarkington returned to Pennsylvania Street in Indianapolis to resume his role as novelist. Motivated somewhat, perhaps, by Maurice Thompson's *Alice of Old Vincennes*, which had been published the previous year, Tarkington turned to early Indiana history as the basis for his next novel. Suggested in part by his mother's memories of her schooldays at St. Mary-of-the-Wood, the plot depends largely upon the experiences of a girl who emerges from behind convent walls into the experiences of the outside world. Some parallels with family history appear (the heroine is named Betty after Tarkington's mother, and she falls in love with a young lawyer modeled somewhat after his father); but, for the most part, *The Two Vanrevels* must be classified as an imaginative, sentimental romance. Following the popular formula, the story is tricked out with another elaborate case of mistaken identity (like that in *Monsieur Beaucaire*) plus a dramatic killing. For the last time for some thirty years, Tarkington had succumbed to the Romantic lure and produced merely another best-seller.

Nevertheless, *The Two Vanrevels* does constitute in some respects a transitional work in Tarkington's career. Had he but capitalized upon his invention, he could have written a solid novel of manners. Terre Haute (Rouen in the novel) at the time of the Mexican War was struggling to retain its proud French culture against the tide of Yankee and Southern migration, and the two generations of Tarkington's tale are perfect foils for such a theme. It is obvious that the young novelist did not realize the potential of his subject, for the social conflict between old and new soon dissolves into "a sentimental melodrama in which Betty's tyrannical father carries on a bitter but unsuccessful feud with his daughter's lover."[25] Only in Tarkington's recognition of material capable of sustaining a novel of manners is there indication that he gradually was stretching beyond the stereotypes of period pieces and was preparing for his later studies of contemporary Midlander life.

## IV   *From Matrimony to Politics*

While Tarkington was working over the closing chapters of *The Two Vanrevels*, rumors of a nonliterary nature concerning him reached the papers, and soon the announcement of a betrothal confirmed the rumors. After eight post-college bachelor years, Tarkington declared himself "ready for marriage." As he had written his friend Dan Calkins, "I have tipped a bishop with infinite grace. I have toasted brides more prettily than you could dream; I have ushered with notable *éclat* and put the cooks of distant relatives in the pew reserved for the groom's mother oftener than any man you know. And I have the weddingest clothes you ever see!"[26] The bride-to-be was Louisa Fletcher, a Smith College graduate ten years Tarkington's junior who shared his interests in drama and literature and who also dabbled in poetry. The two had met as co-actors during the production of *David Garrick* by the Indianapolis Dramatic Club; an intermittent courtship of about a year and a half ensued, and they were married on June 18, 1902.

Following a leisurely honeymoon, the Tarkingtons returned to Indianapolis to a new career for the bridegroom: he became a politician. Months before the wedding, Tarkington had allowed his name to be entered in the Republican primary for State Representative. Much to everyone's surprise, for he had conducted no campaign, he not only won the nomination handily but also the November election. Two months later he took his seat for the opening session in early January, and he attended faithfully until the Assembly adjourned in March. Secretly, Tarkington was elated by the turn of events. Not only had politics always played an important role in the Tarkington family, but his own social conscience was awakening to "the shame of the cities," as Lincoln Steffens phrased it. Most of all, Tarkington sensed that the world of politics might afford him a new region to investigate for novelistic purposes. Weary of costume romances, he already had explored the impact of urbanization in an abortive play and several short stories; in none of them, however, was politics more than a peripheral factor.

The legislative session of 1903 was a revealing, challenging experience for the naïve politico. Contrary to party expectations, he jumped immediately into the political fray. Before the first month was out, he found himself battling Governor Winfield Durbin over a bill to reorganize the state reformatory at Jeffersonville and on the outs with fellow Republicans because of his support of the Sunday Baseball Bill. He won his skirmish against the governor, but legalized Sunday baseball in Indiana waited until 1909. Throughout the session, both as participant and observer, Tarkington was appalled by the political chicanery he noted on every side and by the constant sacrifice of principles to political expediency. Something of a maverick himself, in his review of the session he urged citizens to get into politics regardless of party preferences and to join forces with any group to keep politics "clean and honest."

The immediate literary result of Tarkington's legislative experience was a group of short stories which appeared serially the next year and was then collected under the title *In the Arena* (1905). Ranging all the way from farce to tragedy, these tales were warmly praised in print by President Theodore Roosevelt and acclaimed in sales by the reading public. Several of them, like "Mrs. Protheroe," are direct products of his days in the General Assembly; others, like "The Aliens," are more the results of after-hour socializing and informal politicking. (The latter, "a story of politics in a tough precinct," is a miniature tragedy reminiscent of Upton Sinclair.) All in all, *In the Arena* was a work of high promise which was never fulfilled.

The hectic legislative session drew heavily upon Tarkington's inner resources. Immediately after adjournment, he and his wife retreated to French Lick, a mineral springs resort in southern Indiana. He went with every intention of continuing his career in politics (already there were rumors he might run for mayor of Indianapolis, though he himself seemed to favor the State Senate). At the health resort, of all places, he contracted a case of typhoid fever which proved nearly fatal. After barely being able to return home in the early stage of the disease, Tarkington lay ill until July. Upon his doctor's advice, he retired from politics to go to "the healthiest place in the United States . . . Kennebunkport, Maine." While convalescing, he made extensive plans for his wife and parents to accompany him on a year-long tour abroad; and the four Tarkingtons embarked in mid-September for England.

Tarkington thus began an absence from the Midlands which stretched well beyond the projected visit. Financially independent because of his current publications and his stage productions, Tarkington reveled in the novelty of affluence and "did his sight-seeing in style." His letters home during the trip are a treasury of lively humor, vivid impressions, and keen observations. Throughout the tour he accumulated *objets d'art* for a private collection which ultimately assumed near museum proportions. In fact, all his life Tarkington was an avid art connoisseur who not only contributed generously to the advancement of art appreciation but also used subjects and personalities from the world of art in numerous works of fiction, such as *Rumbin Galleries* (1937) and *Image of Josephine* (1945).

His accounts of this first European trip related many diverting experiences, but they were not of the type which eventuates in serious literature; nor could they have been. After all, his was a holiday junket, not a study tour; Tarkington was primarily concerned with regaining his health. It was impossible, however, for such experiences not to leave many a scene etched on his memory; and his writings hereafter return upon frequent occasions to British and Continental settings. As a matter of fact, the first work that Tarkington produced soon after his return in August 1904 was a two-part tale for *Harper's Weekly* inspired by an incident during his Paris sojourn. Although a minor work, *The Beautiful Lady* is a cleverly plotted *nouvelle* which borrowed a bit from the current interest in the international novel of Howells and James.

Tarkington's principal efforts that autumn went into the dramatization of *The Gentleman from Indiana*. Following the familiar pattern which persists today of adapting a work well known in one form into some other form to capitalize on its popularity, he came up with a script which delighted producer George Tyler. Immediately tryouts were held, a cast was named, and the labor began. From the start, the play was beset with perplexities that no amount of "tinkering" seemed to remedy. "We found it had only read well," Tyler recalled years later; "it just plain wouldn't rehearse." Even when the play opened to a friendly home-town audience in Indianapolis, it bogged down sadly before the final curtain fell. A later attempt in Boston fared no better, and finally the play was dropped.

Despite the failure of the dramatization of *The Gentleman from Indiana*, the year 1905 was a prosperous one for Tarkington. His residence in New York coincided with that period which has been tagged "the golden age" of the mass-produced monthly magazine. Through the competitive efforts of the Periodical Publishers Association, Tarkington found ready sale for whatever came from his pen. In addition, through the social functions sponsored by this association, Tarkington formed alliances with fellow writers and publishers which persisted the rest of his life.

Perhaps the most memorable of these friendships resulted from his very first outing with the association. This was a dinner party at Lakewood, New Jersey, at which he shared a suite with Harry Leon Wilson of *Ruggles of Red Gap* fame, George Lorimer of the *Saturday Evening Post*, and apostate Hoosier novelist David Graham Phillips. Tarkington's relationship with Lorimer during the latter's thirty-eight years as editor of the *Post* provided the fictionist with a lucrative market that seldom failed, and Tarkington responded with a long list of contributions which helped Lorimer to send the circulation of the *Post* to over three million. However, the spontaneous friendship which sprang up between Tarkington and Wilson played an even more significant part in the immediate literary career of Tarkington. During the overnight train trip to Lakewood, the two men laid plans for an informal collaboration which resulted in ten plays. To get their projects under way, Tarkington proposed that they should go to Capri where they might work together without the social pressures of New York, and Wilson agreed.

This venture was delayed because, earlier that spring, Tarkington had begun *The Conquest of Canaan*, a poor-boy-makes-good tale in which the underdog theme was a built-in guarantee of public acceptance. Because of the legal complications that thread the plot, Tarkington drew upon his father for advice as deadlines neared; afterwards he resolved, "Never again a lawyer hero for me." The sale by *Harper's* of seventy thousand copies in the first six weeks did no harm to the Tarkington exchequer, but in his later years the author regarded the work as "a pretty jejune performance." Succeeding generations still find *The Conquest of Canaan* a very readable novel, despite its overdrawn characters and its heavy plot.

In early autumn, the Tarkingtons and the Wilsons set sail for Italy, where they had rented jointly a new villa on the Isle of Capri. In theory, it was an ideal hideaway for artistic creativity—"no newspapers, no autos, no subway, and no telephones to break in upon the tranquillity,"[27] as Tarkington wrote back—but, in practice, he found he was unable to write anything at all. After four months he explained to his bewildered parents, "I pumped the cistern dry last year, I suppose,"[28] although he did not seem concerned. As he had on his Continental tour, Tarkington found Capri wholly delightful; he surrendered himself to its charms, to a vigorous outdoor life, and to making new friends.

It would be unkind to ascribe to Harry Leon Wilson the postponement of Tarkington's major career from 1905 to 1911, although certainly he was a contributing factor. The real reason was that the lure of the theater had become irresistible for Tarkington, and he was determined "to give playwriting a try." During these six years of intense preoccupation with the stage, he produced only one novel (*The Guest of Quesnay*). At the risk of seeming condescension, it must be admitted that none of these theatrical enterprises advanced the status of American drama. Each product of collaboration with Wilson was either a sentimental melodrama or a boisterous farce. *The Man from Home*, their most successful collaboration, was a rollicking burlesque of the American "innocent abroad" which became a minor classic of its kind and a major money-maker. Ironically, it was also the trivial nature of this play and its lack of literary merit which proved to Tarkington his basic unfitness for drama and turned him back to fiction.

Like Henry James before him and Sinclair Lewis after him, Tarkington had to learn for himself the pitfalls of the theater. In the early years of this period no playwright ever enjoyed his labors more than Tarkington. He delighted in all aspects of a theatrical presentation. We should add that Tarkington mastered the craft of playwriting perhaps better than most of his fellow novelists because he regarded the author as only one-third of a team which also included the actors and director— an attitude that enabled him to accept advice willingly and to make revisions cheerfully. After several peripatetic years, however, Tarkington's interest in the stage began to wane. His frequent travels took him from Louisa and their new daughter, Laurel; his mother had died suddenly during one absence; four dramatic failures sapped his strength and drained his resources. In a rare mood of dejection he wrote to his friend Calkins from Indianapolis in 1909: "I'm tired of crossing back and forth, more tired of N. Y.; if I can save a little I'm going to get a few acres in the country near here, build a little shack and settle down."[29]

## V  *The Years of Crisis*

Other reasons for dejection began to fester, although these were never manifested in his correspondence. By the time another year had dragged by, Tarkington's marriage was near an end; his fictional output had dropped to absolute zero; and, as 1910 drew to a close, the only thing that had gone up was his intake of alcohol. When sober, Tarkington was the prince of companions; when in his cups, he became the clown of the party. Unlike Sinclair Lewis, in whose biography Mark Schorer details Lewis's drinking habits in forty-six separate episodes, Tarkington never turned vicious or sour even after heavy drinking. In the innocent years, Tarkington had regarded liquor as "the infinite source of comedy"; but, as 1910 faded, the comic element in alcohol became less and less effective in raising Tarkington above the mounting tragedy in his life.

During that next year Tarkington descended to the lowest level in his artistic, his physical, even his spiritual fortunes. In the early months his marital situation became so unbearable that he could not write, and at midsummer he and Louisa separated. Although a couple of his plays were still alive and his book sales continued, the home town stood ready to abandon him. In July 1911 Tarkington finally escaped with his brother-in-law and his nephew, Ovid and John Jameson, for a two-month auto tour of Europe. In the meantime, to his chagrin, Louisa brought suit for divorce on the grounds of cruelty. In post-Victorian America, no stronger condemnation of a man could be envisioned than the ignominy of divorce upon such a charge; and Tarkington felt the blow keenly. Only after the granting of the divorce on November 13, 1911, was his self-respect regained. Upon that occasion Louisa signed a statement acquitting her former husband of any "unintentional unkindness to me" and also declared that "The differences between us are of temperament and habit, and, after nine years of effort, it is apparent to both of us that we cannot reconcile our views of life."[30]

The dreary months following the divorce were ones of lonely readjustment in the old homestead on North Pennsylvania Avenue. Although Tarkington's father and sister lived nearby, he preferred to remain alone in the familiar house, surrounded by "the kindest ghosts in the world." Throughout his early years, Tarkington had been a social drinker with a fabulous capacity; but he now recognized himself to be a compulsive drinker. As he reviewed the situation much later, "I suddenly decided

I preferred to die sober. Got so I craved a drink before breakfast. . . . But as it turned out, it required surprisingly little will power to climb aboard the wagon. Couple of days later I was in the University Club and a fellow asked me to have a drink. I took one whiff and it smelled like kerosene. That was that."[31]

The fact of the matter is that he drank himself into a severe heart seizure which sent him to bed for several weeks—although the rest of his Twainlike tale may be true. In all probability a little essay called "Nipskillions," published in 1916, gives a rather accurate account of his own final bout with drink. Like Tarkington himself, the narrator concludes: "I knew I couldn't drink moderately. I didn't want to drink moderately. I wanted to drink immoderately—enough for comedy, a hearty laugh, not a mere little smile of quiet exhilaration. . . . So I made up my mind, not that I would quit but that I *had* quit."[32]

CHAPTER *4*

# The Industrial Age

$A$FTER the ground-haze of matrimonial distress had lifted and the blur of incipient alcoholism had cleared by late 1911, Tarkington took a long look about him for the first time since his return from eight years first of European expatriation and then of theatrical barnstorming. He found that he had come back to a Midwest quite different from the idyllic region of his youthful memories. As Woodress observes: "No longer could he appraise Indiana uncritically as he once did in *The Gentleman from Indiana,* for he saw with alarm that everywhere about him people worshipped materialism, bigness, and speed. The sedate, well-mannered, and self-contained society that he remembered in Indianapolis in 1900 had crumbled before the irresistible force of big business and the vast complexities of an industrial America."[1]

## I  *The Chronicler of Change*

As Tarkington pondered the evidence of change about him, two basic concepts evolved which came to dominate much of the major phase of his writing. The first of these was a firm conviction that constructive growth is an essential ingredient of a healthy economy. Whereas change for the sake of change seemed downright foolhardy to Tarkington, he upheld any technological advancement which promised social amelioration. "The world does move," he was wont to say; the wise man learns not only to accept the inevitability of change but to capitalize on it. With dogged optimism, Tarkington insisted that the sociological and ecological problems of industrialism eventually would be solved. "The kiln must be fired before the vase is glazed,"
58

he pointed out to skeptics of capitalistic democracy during the Depression; though presently vexed with the "turmoil" of "growth" (two Tarkington terms), he was convinced that America would move ahead into a New Age of enlightened prosperity. The sooty smoke of the Sheridan Pump Works in *The Turmoil* can be minimized by proper controls and by a protective "green belt"; the tenement blight of urbanization can be averted by transit lines into the rolling hills of the Ornaby Addition in *The Midlander*. As a staunch Republican, Tarkington upheld a long tradition of national progressivism rooted deep in a capitalistic society.

The other product of his observations was the realization that change wears several garbs. To one, it may come as a welcome step toward a brighter future; to another, as an alarming threat to comfortable security. To some, change may seen a promising approach to a vexatious issue; to others, an ominous move toward certain disaster. No matter what the variant attitudes might be, however, Tarkington sensed that they breed the drama, the conflicts, the tensions of powerful fiction. In one form or another, the polemics of change were to provide him with the material from which he drew his richest novels.

Tarkington's own position toward socio-economic change was that of the practical idealist. Although he envisioned to the last a better and brighter United States, he never denied the core of materialism in the American Dream. In much the same way as he included economic reward in his concept of the successful novelist, he incorporated ample creature comforts, social intercourse, and cultural opportunities in his concept of the good life. As a practicalist, there is his acceptance of "things," of the material, in a utilitarian sense; as an idealist, however, he insisted upon the esthetic, even the spiritual. "Neither is good nor fair alone"; their happy combination in proper proportions, Tarkington felt, makes for the most rewarding living. Even in his chosen field, Tarkington was no literary ascetic. Tempted though he had been by the lures of Parisian culture, he found nothing attractive about a cold-water walkup flat in the Latin Quarter or about a garret in Montmartre.

To Tarkington's eye, American materialism is still unfinished business. Too often it is merely the "Bigness" of *The Turmoil,* the "Boost, Don't Knock!" of *The Midlander.* It is that partial vision which identifies quantity with quality, which confuses glitter with glow: the John Hancock Building versus the spires of Oxford, Disneyland versus Salzburg. In its most insidious form, Tarkington felt, materialism in the United States is a manifestation of a force more subtle and more profound than a taste for bigness and brashness: it means complacency toward life which does not distinguish between the timely and the timeless, the worldly and the spiritual, between matter and mind. Somehow the artist must point out this deficiency in the American mystique, and to this end Tarkington devoted the most creative years of his career.

Although not wholly successful in every instance, Tarkington did paint a series of remarkable portraits personifying this aspect of the American scene. Ranging from the Sheridan family of *The Turmoil* to the Amberson dynasty of *The Magnificent Ambersons,* these men from industry and business typify a persistent Tarkington ideal—the blending of the visionary and the workman into the full man. There are sacrifices to be made, there are losses for the gains, but the final result is a massive figure of heroic mold. Like Dan Oliphant of *The Midlander,* he may not survive to see his dreams fulfilled; but it is made abundantly clear by Tarkington that others have caught Dan's vision and that his good work will continue.

## II  The Turmoil: *The Pains of Growth*

From January to March, in 1914, Tarkington sat long hours at the drawing table he used for a desk and poured out *The Turmoil,* the first volume of a trilogy entitled *Growth,* which developed during the ensuing decade. Briefly, *The Turmoil* is the story of a first-generation ascendancy to wealth at the sacrifice of second-generation aspirations to culture. In a number of respects, the novel is similar to *The Rise of Silas Lapham* by William Dean Howells. Although a bigger frog in a smaller puddle, James Sheridan of the Sheridan Pump Works in Indianapolis is cousin-german to Silas Lapham, the paint tycoon of Boston in the Howells novel. Both men are self-made, self-righteous successes who are constructed by their creators in full accordance with the historic American prescription for success. Both men soar to the heights in their business deals, but they flounder in the furrows of their domestic affairs.

By the end of their careers, however, a marked divergence in their development appears: Lapham suffers economic catastrophe, only to "rise" a bigger man from experience; Sheridan undergoes a series of tragic shocks, but the Pump Company ultimately thrives under the firm control of his re-created son. Tarkington makes it clear that Sheridan senior creates his own problems in his attempts to run his family like an industrial enterprise. The author leaves no doubt in the reader's mind that in so doing the father sacrifices his favorite son on the altar of business. When he forces a second son into the business, he cracks under the double strain of parental coercion and marital trouble. Sheridan senior even dismisses an unacceptable suitor for his daughter, only to precipitate an unhappy elopement. Bibbs Sheridan alone, the last of three sons (and, as a would-be poet, obviously considered the least as well), can shape himself under duress into the parental mold.

Thus far, *The Turmoil* appears to be a scathing denunciation of the high-handed financier who should "get his come-uppance" in the next-to-the-last chapter. Indeed, one critic declared upon the publication of the novel that "Tarkington pulled no punches in attacking the scramble for wealth." The truth of the matter may be somewhat at variance with this judgment; indeed, Tarkington himself had misgivings about the power of his work. "Commercialization is the savage of the world," he wrote a friend while the novel was being serialized; "it's that stinking dirty brute I'm after, with what entrails I have, in *The Turmoil*, which is written much more feebly than I'd like."[2]

Within the early pages of *The Turmoil*, the first act of a drama unfolds in which the male leads, industrialist James Sheridan and his poet son Bibbs, personify two conflicting elements in twentieth-century America—Mammon and Art. As it turns out, the engagement soon turns into a minor skirmish; in the closing pages, Art is in full rout. Tarkington does not imply undue sacrifice when the young man lays his charred sheaf of dreams upon the altar of Bigness to become an acolyte to his father. And perhaps the son's sacrifice is not too great; at least, a wily Tarkington extenuates the situation by having Bibbs confess, "I've never written anything worth printing, and I never shall." His fiancée, Mary Vertrees, protests, "But I *know* you could! Ah, it's a pity life won't let you!" Again the young man does not hesitate: "It isn't," said Bibbs honestly. "I never could."[3] Having very little evidence upon which to base his own conclusion, the reader must accept the judgment of the would-be poet. Bibbs is an attractive young man who is loved by a sweet, wholesome girl; and the reader must sympathize with his forfeiture of artistic aspirations. Yet Tarkington did not regard his creation as a tragic figure. As Woodress affirms, "The transformation of Bibbs from poet to industrialist is not tragic, for Tarkington has no tragic sense, and in addition sees his character as fulfilling a historic role in capitalistic society."[4]

Perhaps it should be made more clear that the transformation of Bibbs is a gradual process in the development of this major theme in *The Turmoil*. Tarkington carefully worked the change into the matrix of the plot in such a way that it acts as motivation for each successive stage. James Sheridan, "the high priest of Bigness," has no delusions about the preeminence of money and the virtue of work. When Bibbs returns from college with nothing but a notebook filled with words (precisely as Tarkington had done), the father realizes that his son needs to learn something about the real world. After an annoying delay caused by illness, the poet is assigned to a shop job typical in its mechanized monotony. With love for Mary Vertrees to speed his fingers, however, Bibbs finds that, even as he labors, his thoughts soar freely; indeed, he feels a strange independence. One evening he comes home and writes in his journal: "Manual labor is best. Your heart can sing and your mind can dream while your hands are working."[5] When Sheridan senior discovers that Bibbs also writes that "You could not have a singing heart and a dreaming mind all day if you had to scheme out dollars, or if you had to add columns of figures," he places his son in an executive position where Bibbs has nothing but dollars and figures to deal with. As the father watches his son's business acumen emerge, he exults, "Why, a year from now I'll bet you he won't know there ever was such a thing as poetry!"[6]

For Bibbs, this statement is sound prophecy. Although Tarkington does not spell out the details, he makes it evident that his young hero will advance the family's business interests and, at the same time, achieve personal satisfaction. When Howells read the novel, he felt that Bibbs was given a fate "too dire for consolation"; Tarkington, as noted above, did not share this sentiment in like degree. *The Turmoil* implies clearly that Bibbs, artist and esthete though he may be, is still smaller than the issues surrounding him. When son yields to father, the act appears as a fitting gesture of family loyalty; when poet yields to entrepreneur, the move rings true as a simple surrender to forces greater than self. *Ars longa, vita brevis,* Tarkington seems to say. The cultural growth of mankind is a long-term process, and each must make his contribution in his own way. By taking a mediocre poet and transforming him into a dynamic executive, Tarkington implies plainly that Bibbs Sheridan has thereby found his assigned role in the greater scheme.

This interpretation of *The Turmoil* by no means prevailed among its early critics. Indeed, the conversion of Bibbs the artist into Bibbs the magnate struck the *literati* as rank treason. British critic R. Ellis Roberts seized upon the novel as a typical example of American abjuration of the intellectual aristocracy in the country's worship of money. "In the States," Roberts declared, "the men who should rule the world become slaves to it. The poet is humble before the plutocrat, and does not think that he does wrong."[7] Quite unknown to him or to Tarkington, the English reviewer provided the American novelist with both thesis and title for a subsequent work entitled *The Plutocrat,* a deceptively simple tale with provocative connotations.

As noted earlier, by Tarkington's own confession, *The Turmoil* is in some respects a disappointing novel. It is impossible, of course, to know the precise implications of his comment that it was "written much more feebly than I'd like." Perhaps Tarkington would have enjoyed rattling the skeletons in the closets of Big Business more vigorously; perhaps he had second thoughts about abandoning his highly autobiographical hero to the ravages of industry. Most likely, however, he regretted his hasty two-month treatment of a complex theme. Indeed, like every other American novelist before and after him, Tarkington encountered a persistent problem in this respect—how can one attack the evils of capitalistic industrialism with one hand while defending its basic societal roles with the other? Clearly, the situation presents a challenge which might daunt the most able campaigner. As a newcomer on the field at the time of *The Turmoil*, Tarkington was unsure about the nature of his opponent and uncertain as to his own strategy—and the novel suffers as a consequence.

The first of these conjectures about Big Business invites explication, for Tarkington devised several variations upon the theme in his mature writings. Like such contemporary novelists as Theodore Dreiser and Sinclair Lewis, he was captivated by the subject but not always certain what to do with it. More and more aware of the industrialization which ultimately engulfed his own home, Tarkington still sheltered a Republicanism which espoused such American traditions as free enterprise, free competition, and free capitalism. As a close companion of moneyed men, even as a modest capitalist in his own right, he was a staunch defender of the American businessman and a sharp reviler of the petty critics who led attacks against him. Some of his sharpest barbs he cast beyond the *Growth* trilogy, particularly in *The Plutocrat*.

On the other hand, Tarkington was himself "a gentleman from Indiana." An esthete by nature, he was reared in a home of comparative refinement and wealth. A *litterateur* by talent and training, he felt only sympathy for the creative artist in a workaday world. From his formative years he was convinced that one of his primary responsibilities as a novelist was to dramatize basic social truths in a style and form best suited to move the greatest number of readers. To some degree a casualty of the cross fire between two persistent antagonists, *The Turmoil* remains Tarkington's first exemplification of that immutable force which ultimately bends the creative soul in society to "the will of the acquisitors."

In fact, the mature Tarkington maintained that the contributions of the machine age to the amelioration of American cultural standards have far surpassed whatever losses they may have caused. In a spirited defense of "Rotarians" (those magnates of Big Business much maligned by the "Sophisticates"), he pointed out that "this satirized American business man has done more important things than to feed, clothe, house, transport and give light, heat and reading to his critics." In addition, he has provided the vision to throw up a vast complex of cities and facilities which have made America foremost in worldwide economy, authority, and prestige. In place after place, Tarkington asserted, "the American business man is responsible for more than the incalculable material progress of the country. The very seats of learning where his critics acquire scholarship exist principally by means of his gifts and endowments; so do the great institutions for scientific and hygienic research, so do countless hospitals and benevolences of every kind; so do libraries, museums, the great collections of the masterpieces in art, schools for the study of the arts, crafts, and professions." In fact, the novelist concluded, "If those rebellious young critics could only realize it, . . . if it weren't for the business man and his gifts and endowments the institutions would not exist at all." With typical disdain toward the carping "intelligentzia [*sic*]," the practical Tarkington thus defended the materialistic money-grubbers. Indeed, he hinted darkly, if the truth be told, were it not for the menial functions of these lowbrow worldlings, hypercritical esthetes might well be "naked, thirsty, dirty and starving and, like civilization, would perish from the earth."[8]

Although the foregoing pronouncements were uttered from the golden heights of Coolidge inflation in 1928, they represent Tarkington's attitudes throughout his life. Perhaps it need not be pointed out that such comments were provoked largely by the persistent defamation of America and Americans from such literary exiles as Ezra Pound and Henry Miller throughout the decade following World War I. Amid the constant barrage of vilification from the expatriates on the Left Bank, Tarkington stood firm in his defense of the United States. A bit later, in March 1929, he reiterated his old position: "The critics have said everything they can, yet all they've made is a little sharp scratching, a little defacement. They have built nothing, while he whom they call the 'Rotarian' has built everything. The critics' scratching is the end of their power, the American business man is but at the beginning of his."[9]

Paul Meadows, writing at mid-century in a study entitled *The Culture of the Industrial Man,* asserts that "contempt for an industrialized society dies hard because it is constantly receiving blood transfusions from an *avant-garde* group of artists and dilettanti alienated from their native culture... in which they have never been at home."[10] Such a coterie of self-appointed carpers Tarkington lumped together as "the Sophisticates," or "the intelligentzia." Referring again to such persons as the contributors to Harold Stearns's *Civilization in the United States: An Inquiry by Thirty Americans* (1922), Tarkington felt that these "esthetic Cassandras" were taking a negative approach in their analysis of contemporary culture in refusing to recognize the positive contributions made by Big Business to "the American way of life." He deplored their unbalanced criticism, their destructive vituperation, and their vociferous disloyalty to hearth and homeland. "To me," he said, "the new sophisticates seem virulent. They mock; they attack; they ridicule; always they seem to look down from a great height, disliking the stupid and petty creature whom they have labeled Rotarian.... He appears in the satirist's joke as the incarnation of all that is pretentious, blatant, cheap and fraudulent. He is the reiteration of endless buncombe; his vocabulary consists of pinchbeck; his patriotism is a telling selfishness; he is a noisy 'go-getter'; he has no virtues, no worth to the world; all in all, he has nothing but his offensiveness."[11]

To this composite image of the American businessman Tarkington objected. Although he had his own reservations about more than a few of the details, a steady confidence in an enlightened capitalistic system appears throughout the Tarkington canon. Even the dour days of the Depression saw him unshaken in this faith at a time when hosts of his fellows were seeking solace in some form of Socialism. In his study of Sinclair Lewis, Mark Schorer points out that "American literature had a rich, if brief, tradition of the business novel. James, Howells, Norris, London, Phillips, Herrick, Sinclair, Wharton, Dreiser, Poole, Tarkington—all these writers had been centrally concerned with the business man."[12] For this study of Tarkington the social critic, it is significant to observe that Schorer adds, "after James and Howells, only Tarkington was to find in him any of the old, perdurable American virtues."[13]

However, Tarkington was not in sympathy with every aspect of industrialization in the United States. To his repatriated eyes, the sooty pall of soft-coal smoke which "hung over the city of Indianapolis like the foul breath of the industrial giant beneath it"[14] was both the despoiler of beauty and the defiler of morality. Through the ten years and four social-criticism novels that mark his major phase, smoke became the dominant symbol of the corruption spread by unrestrained, unrestricted commercialism. In *The Turmoil*, Tarkington's initial study of the changing scene, James Sheridan could stand outside his factory, watch the soot settle upon his white shirt-cuffs, even touch it to his tongue, and exclaim, "It's good! It's good! Good, clean soot: it's our life-blood, God bless it!"[15] To the housewives who would lift the blight, he replied, "Smoke's what brings your husbands' money home on Saturday night."[16] To Sheridan, the smoke was a symbol not only of his own fortune but of the prosperity of the community; to Tarkington in 1914, this same smoke was an ominous symbol of an insidious new clause in the city's revised catechism: "Wealth! I will get Wealth! I will make Wealth! I will sell Wealth for more Wealth! My house shall be dirty, my garment shall be dirty, and I will foul my neighbor so that he cannot be clean—but I will get Wealth!"[17]

## III   The Magnificent Ambersons: *The Promising Alliance*

Four years later, in *The Magnificent Ambersons* (1918), smoke returns as a symbol of the blight which creeping industrialism can inflict upon a community and its citizens. In this three-tiered study of the shifting socio-economic scene in post-bellum mid-America, Major Amberson typifies the doomed gentility of the older generation. His daughter's would-be suitor, Eugene Morgan, is a pioneer automobile manufacturer who represents brawny (and brainy) business in the new age of hustle. The Major's grandson, George Minafer, emerges in the third generation to personify through his marriage with Lucy Morgan the happy wedding of the old graces with the new dynamism. Neither of these developments, however, comes easily or early. Through the vicissitudes of his limited cast of characters, Tarkington dramatizes with ruthless candor the growth pains that afflict an industrialized society during its adolescent years.

Change is always hardest for the established. By Midwestern standards, the three generations of "magnificent Ambersons" at the turn of the century constituted a dynasty of Victorian gentility to which other citizens paid unquestioning homage. The family name graced the principal avenue of the Midland city, the family mansion dominated the residential section, and the family's hospitality dictated the social calendar. The title of the novel reflects the corrosive irony of the situation, but Tarkington also generates powerful pathos in *The Magnificent Ambersons*. The reader is swept into a maze of mixed loyalties. Much as he may denounce the Major as a shrewd robber baron, much as he may scorn the Major's son-in-law as a boneless parasite who should never have been let into the family, much as he may detest young George as a spoiled brat long overdue for his "come-uppance," he cannot deny a profound respect for the Amberson dynasty which had come so far from so little. Neither can he suppress some twinge of regret when the old order passes and a new, unpredictable generation assumes control.

During the descent of the Ambersons, as the factories sprawl apace and the smoke-cloud darkens, the Major becomes increasingly fearful about the future. Day by day he watches the proliferation of uncontrolled industrialism engulf his home, transform his apartments into tenements, and drive his grandchildren into the country ("suburb" was yet to be invented). Such is to be the path of progress, Morgan the entrepreneur warns the old man; "soon the automobile is going to carry city streets clear out to the country line."[18] At the time, Major Amberson decries such heresy. "It's lucky for us that you're only dreaming," he tells Morgan; "because if people go to moving that far, real estate values in the old residence parts of town are going to be stretched pretty thin."[19] Both prophecy and rejoinder prove true. For the Ambersons (and for thousands like them across America), this vision of Eugene Morgan turns into a nightmare during which they see both name and fortune sink into near oblivion.

Blessed with a hindsight denied the Ambersons, Tarkington does not leave this drab prospect without some glimmer of hope. Again, his practical idealism is expressed by the industrialist. Speaking semi-seriously, Morgan assures the Major that the situation need not become desperate, provided "you keep things so bright and clean that the old section will stay more attractive than the new one." In his response, Amberson reveals his growing pessimism. "Not very likely!" he exclaims. "How are things going to be kept 'bright and clean' with soft coal and our kind of government?" A dual question begets a double answer, so Morgan replies, "Abolish the smoke and get a new kind of city government."[20] Sensing at this point that he is suggesting prospective moves to a retrospective listener, Morgan temporarily shelves his idealism for a bit of immediate advice. In view of impending disaster, he urges that the sensible move for Amberson is "to take warning in time," dispose of his property at its best price, then retreat "to the country." To surrender the field thus early in the fray is unthinkable to the old soldier, and the warfare of change grinds on.

The battle is a futile and a pathetic one, for no one family could stem the relentless drive. Bastion after bastion falls until the defeat is final. As the novel closes, George Minafer "made one of his Sunday walks into a sour pilgrimage." Along its route he finds that both the Amberson Hotel and Amberson Opera House have been razed for a great department store, the "Amberson Block" has become "Doogan's Storage," both the Mansion and the Major's apartments have given way to a sprawling tenement, Amberson Boulevard is now Tenth Street, and the new "Civic History" makes no mention of the family name. "The city had rolled over the Ambersons and buried them under to the last vestige."[21] Not quite all is lost, for the optimism of Tarkington draws together the remnants of this tragic devastation at the close of the novel. Through the marriage of George Amberson and Lucy Morgan, Tarkington implies, a finer generation compounded of the best of the old and the new will arise.

*The Magnificent Ambersons,* of course, holds a unique place in the Tarkington story, for it is the first of his two novels to win the Pulitzer Prize. With rare consensus, critics agree that this well-wrought novel is "a book to conjure with." Within the tight confines of what Howells called "the intensive style," Tarkington maneuvered the lives of but two families through three generations to depict a major upheaval in the American social order. In part, this triple structure was designed to dramatize a frequent phenomenon observed by Tarkington whereby families in the United States pass in three generations "from rags to riches to near rags again." Of greater import, however, is the interplay between moribund gentility and upstart plutocracy. The fatal flaws of the Amberson character are its incapacity to recognize growth and its inability to accept change. In a desperate effort to sustain the past, the family is but barely aware of the present—and it has no concept of the future. On the other side, Eugene Morgan is a successful entrepreneur because he looks constantly from the present toward the future. "Whirl is king," said Aristophanes over two thousand years ago, and woe to the laggards. Tarkington would have agreed completely.

## IV  The Midlander: *The Party of Vision*

Tarkington was obviously intrigued by this theme of socio-economic change in early twentieth-century America; for his third novel in the *Growth* trilogy, *The Midlander* (1924), also uses the smoke-laden air of the mid-city as a motivating symbol. Soon it becomes evident, however, that a reinterpretation must be made. As this novel develops, a subtle alchemy transforms those ugly columns of sooty smoke into twining plumes of beauty. The miracle is wrought largely by Dan Oliphant, the young protagonist of *The Midlander,* who pits his vision of a burgeoning suburbia against the rigid traditions of urban life. Investing all his money and energy in the development of the Ornaby Addition, Dan fights with Rotarian zeal for streetcar lines to permit shop-workers to escape the tenements, for zoning ordinances to confine the unavoidable ugliness of industry, and for more realistic legislation on loans and mortgages to enable the small wage-earner to buy his own home.

To the Midlander, Ornaby Addition is a residential area rich in the potential beauty of green grass and white cottages. It symbolizes a whole new way of life for the city-dweller who may never have known the purity of fresh-fallen snow or the loveliness of spring bloom. But, like the Tarkington of 1924, Dan Oliphant also recognizes the dependence of an abundant society upon a prosperous industrialized economy. As his assistant explains to Dan's skeptical brother Harlan, "I think the smoke's beautiful to him because he believes it means growth and power, and he thinks they're beautiful."[22]

Although Dan becomes, like Bibbs Sheridan in *The Turmoil*, an early sacrifice to the progressivism of his time, he lives long enough to see the realization of his dreams. Appropriately enough, the first family to build in the new subdivision is that of a man whose "house was far down in the city where the smoke had begun to discourage his wife." Ornaby Addition does get its transit line, more and more families succumb to the lures of suburbia ("Every Ornaby Buyer Is An Ornaby Booster!"), and Dan himself, who has built in the new development, is finally joined by his entire family.

But this accomplishment is not to be an easy victory, as Dan soon learns. Vested "downtown" interests oppose him because they fear, not without reason, that peripheral expansion may well endanger the value of their holdings. Local merchants oppose him because they envision, with accuracy, the siphoning of their established business into new areas. City officials oppose him because they see in the Addition nothing but more responsibilities for their maintenance departments. The older residents, like the Major in *The Magnificent Ambersons*, oppose him because they fear the depreciation of their homes. Even Harlan Oliphant, Dan's brother, has nothing but harsh words for the project and finds only misfortune in the city's growth. To Martha, his wife-to-be, he complains, "To my mind it's only an extension of hideousness, and down where I live, in my grandmother's old house, it's getting so smoky in winter that the air is noxious—the whole town's dirty, for that matter." At first Martha can only agree, for she has barely returned from Europe. "Yes," she says, "yesterday, as soon as I got here, I noticed that even in the summer the air's smokier than it used to be. I think the city was a cleaner place and a better-looking place when I went away."[23]

Even as she speaks, however, tiny doubts arise. She recalls that, as she was driven home, "some of these long, wide streets are pleasant, even to a person who's stayed in Europe too long perhaps." Martha soon detects that "a change has begun," just as Tarkington had when he returned to Indianapolis after his *Wanderjahre.* To a querulous Harlan she finally declares, "I believe it's the growth—I think it's the incredible growth that Dan predicted."[24] Martha is right: the "growth" that pervades this Tarkington trilogy has indeed come. At the close of *The Midlander,* as Martha and Harlan stand on their terrace overlooking Ornaby Addition, "there, against the evening blue, the thinning end of a plume of smoke, miles long, was visible. 'Do you find even that beautiful?' he asks. 'Dan must have thought so,' she says. 'I think,' Harlan concedes, 'I think maybe he did.'"[25]

The last paragraph of these three long novels clearly indicates that Tarkington, too, "felt something in it" which he had not sensed in *The Turmoil* ten years earlier. It is not without significance that the final scene of *The Midlander* leaves the reader "still looking up at the smoke against the sky, so far above the long masses of flowering bridal wreath that bordered the terrace." Smoke in the sky, bloom along the terrace—each has its own peculiar beauty. Even as Bibbs Sheridan became reconciled to the strident turmoil of Big Business, so Tarkington came to accept the ugliness of industry in exchange for its benefits. The formula is by no means so simple as one novel can detail, but the basic concept is to keep in control the unavoidable dirt and din of factories and foundries; to remember that the security of prosperity comes from their productivity; and, at the same time, to set aside residential areas well apart from the commercial zone provided with "transit lines and bridal wreath." In essence, this is *The Midlander*—smoke in the sky; bloom along the terrace.

## V  The Plutocrat: *The New Roman*

Only three years after *The Midlander,* the impetus of *Growth* led Tarkington to create one of his most delightful novels,

*The Plutocrat.* Its title might well have been *The Midlander Abroad,* for the inconsequential plot closely follows the first portion of a six-month European tour which Tarkington himself had taken a year earlier. Bordering on a burlesque of Mark Twain at times, verging upon the "democratic vista" of Walt Whitman at others, *The Plutocrat* purports to take a Midwestern businessman, his wife, and their daughter on a typical cruise. Much of the activity takes place aboard the *Duumvir* en route to North Africa; and much more is based on Tarkington's own trip by motorcar from Algiers to Tunis and then by boat to Sicily.

Although there is ample hilarity in the novel, much of the *Duumvir's* lading is satire. Exercising freely the prerogatives of the satirist, Tarkington composed his passenger list with gleeful malice. With few exceptions, everybody is something: an artist, a critic, an industrialist, a poet—whatever Tarkington at that time felt needed attack or defense. Aware that such a scattering of targets might disconcert his readers, he supplied the rudiments of a story: a setting, the Atlantic Ocean and points southeast; a plot, consisting of a very tepid romance; and a protagonist, one Earl Tinker.

Tinker, of course, is "the Plutocrat"; although he is known variously in the course of the novel as "the new Roman," "the Great Yawp," and "the Rotarian." By dint of native shrewdness and persevering labor, Earl Tinker has become president of the Illinois and Union Paper Company. We may detect in his name two attributes which Tarkington ascribes to him: "Earl," a noble title indicative of leadership; and "Tinker," a familiar label suggestive of practical ingenuity. And what a formidable plutocrat is Mr. Tinker as he showers his largesse with vast good-humor wherever he goes. A stroll through a bazaar with him is suddenly a parade; an afternoon side-trip becomes a safari.

Loud-mouthed, uncouth, ill-mannered, the plutocrat epitomizes to the casual observer all the grossness of the provincial American tourist. To the Sophisticates aboard the *Duumvir,* of course, he is the ultimate in vulgarity. Gradually, however, we realize that Tinker is the embodiment of what Henry Seidel Canby identified as "the brash, self-confident American, who used to snap his fingers at the world." Writing but six years after Tinker's appearance at the crest of Coolidge inflation (and four years into the depths of Hoover depression), Canby bemoaned the loss of such stalwarts on the national scene who so recently were "the heroes in most of the novels and short stories about America." Nostalgically, Canby recalls that "Booth Tarkington did him beautifully in *The Plutocrat*, crude, noisy, afraid of nothing but the wife, self-assured, with a reserve of power that came from a deep self-confidence."[26]

Tinker assuredly is caricature bred by satire, but he must not be regarded as merely a clown or a clod. As a matter of fact, Tarkington drew much of the man from his traveling companion on a similar junket, Howard Fisher of Pittsburgh. Woodress reports, "Fisher's uninhibited response to things foreign and his unabashed Americanness, in primitive Arab villages as well as in luxurious hotels, delighted Tarkington."[27] He merely capitalized on the comic aspects of Fisher for the humorous episodes with which the book is filled. The real significance of Earl Tinker lies in Tarkington's representation of him as "a modern Roman"; for this industrialist from the American Midwest is to be interpreted as a reincarnation of the empire-building genius which created "the grandeur that was Rome." Lifted by the tides of history from the Old World, this protean figure now assumes his pioneering role in shaping the destiny of the New. Indeed, in multifarious details, Tinker springs directly from the hortatory lines of Walt Whitman's paeans of patriotism. Throughout *The Plutocrat*, he sounds his "barbaric yawp," out-shouting "the brag" of ancient Rome in his exuberant love for lusty, young America.

Indeed, the archeologist who lectures to the tourist trade at Timgad, Algeria, perceives the affinity between Tinker, the modern Roman, and his prototype of old. "You think perhaps the Romans didn't have their brag?" Dr. Medjila exclaims to Lawrence Ogle, the hypercritic of culture in his native United States. "Heavens! What braggarts! You find the imperial Roman Yawp in thousands of inscriptions everywhere—everywhere! America has so much that is the same as these dead people: the great Yawp, the love of health, the love of plumbing, the

love of power, of wealth, and above all, the worship of bigness—
that old, old passion for giantism."[28]

Bigness—here that word from *The Turmoil* is used with a
new significance. Once the synonym for gross materialism in
a jerry-built American culture, bigness in *The Plutocrat* implies
Tarkington's ultimate trust in paternalistic capitalism, his confidence in "the American way." Like the plutocrat's forebears
of old, Tinker "knew how to lay out and build a town, and
the Romans had done it the same way *he* would—only not
so good!"[29] By extension, the entrepreneurs of America are
even more capable of plotting out a new culture than were
their counterparts of the Augustan Age. As Woodress expresses
it, "The Tinkers of Illinois, as the Romans before them, are
empire-builders, organizers, braggarts, and Rotarians."[30] The
only difference between the ancient architect of Timgad and
the manufacturer from Illinois is the opportunity of the latter
to have the last brag.

Despite deprecatory murmurs from its author and its heavy
camouflage of humorous satire, *The Plutocrat* must stand as
Tarkington's supreme glorification of the American businessman
and as his defense of American capitalism. In typical offhand
fashion, Tarkington himself explained, "My fellow is a big,
bragging Illinois manufacturer—he gets drunk, lies to his wife,
chases women, makes himself a spectacle, and is a real show,
I think."[31] It is true that Tinker does all these things; yet,
because of him, the work is raised to the level of serious social
criticism. To dismiss Earl Tinker as either a bumpkin or a
boor is to defeat the central purpose of the novel and to dilute
its satire into the slapstick of burlesque. Beneath his façade of
naïveté, the protagonist is a "tinker"—a maker and a mender.
In his obtuse fashion, the plutocrat is Tarkington's messenger
of faith in our American blend of creative genius, practical
progressivism, and humanitarian generosity.

## VI The Heritage of Hatcher Ide: *Testament of Faith*

To the end of his long career, Tarkington maintained much
the same attitude of optimism toward an evolving American
economy. During the last years of his life, he returned from

various literary excursions to the scene of his ripest creative period—his native Indiana. Late in 1939 he began composing *The Heritage of Hatcher Ide,* which brought the Midland family sagas of the *Growth* trilogy to the eve of World War II. Despite the novel's contemporary setting, there is much in it that is reminiscent of an earlier day. "It awakened a melancholy streak in me," wrote his Princeton roommate, Harold Murray; "*The Turmoil, The Magnificent Ambersons* and *The Man of the Family* [as *The Heritage* was titled in serial form] all dovetail together."[32] In this novel, Tarkington evoked a familiar world, one with the same roots and traditions which underlie the earlier tales of the Sheridans and the Ambersons.

The "melancholy" of Harold Murray is by no means the dominant tone set by the seventy-two-year-old novelist in *The Heritage of Hatcher Ide.* Its young hero, thrust from college in late Depression years, must turn to grubby rent-collecting to eke out a living. How Hatcher transforms the run-down houses under his charge into productive real estate is Tarkington's final affirmation of faith "in the regeneration of America by her youth." When John P. Marquand reviewed the novel, he said in conclusion that "there is the same vigor and the same unerring eye for detail that is present in all of his other pages and, best of all, there is that spirit of optimism, that unconquerable glow of hope in Mr. Tarkington's young . . . which raises it above its worldly plot and which lightens its shadows; and all this is done in a manner which is beyond the power of any other living novelist."[33]

Marquand's concluding clause is high praise from a fellow novelist—probably too high for most critics. Nevertheless, we must agree with Woodress that "*The Heritage of Hatcher Ide* is perhaps Tarkington's best late novel, a well-constructed piece of fiction with depth and breadth."[34] There is a solidity in characterization and a control of plot which one sometimes misses in the lighter novels of his middle years. Aside from its stylistic competence, however, it should be emphasized that the book is an example of unrelieved Realism. Indeed, when it appeared in the *Saturday Evening Post,* the editors feared it might be "too depressing for their readers." Yet the final note is not tragic, despite the suicide of Hatcher's uncle and the defection of the young man's love interest. Tarkington makes it clear that "the new generation is left afloat after their elders flounder in the economic storm."[35]

## VII *The Social Novels: An Afterview*

By common critical consent, these socio-economic studies of mid-America in transition constitute Tarkington's most important contributions to American letters. Through the *Growth* trilogy, *The Plutocrat*, *The Heritage of Hatcher Ide*, as well as a sprinkling of related titles, Tarkington expressed steady faith in the American dream of social betterment, the American scheme of free enterprise, and the American theme of optimistic progressivism. Although he found it increasingly difficult to preserve the delicate balance between practicality and idealism, Tarkington clung to his basic convictions during two world wars and a major depression.

Tarkington's own career exemplifies this deliberate compromise in a most fitting manner. As John P. Marquand expressed it, "By his own unvarying standards and good taste he proved that literature can be produced outside of an ivory tower and sold in the market-place."[36] Twice winner of the Pulitzer Prize (in 1919 for *The Magnificent Ambersons*, in 1922 for *Alice Adams*), recipient of the William Dean Howells Medal of the American Academy of Arts and Letters (in 1945 for *Image of Josephine*), and receiver of numerous other literary honors, Tarkington needs no defense for his literary distinction. He also needs little introduction as one of our most successful writers in the monetary sense of the term. As a biographical sketch in a recent reissue of *The Magnificent Ambersons* remarks, "He is one of the few American writers to have become wealthy exclusively from writing." For his affluence he made no apology; rather, he used his wealth like the patron of old for the advancement of culture. Great art may sometimes be the product of pain, he admitted; but more often, he insisted, it is the product of security. He was convinced that an enlightened capitalism might thus make its most significant contribution to an environment of creativity.

As noted in later pages, these novels of social concern also reflect the serious craftsman in such fundamental areas as characterization and literary style. Together with *Alice Adams*, they exemplify the type of "selective Realism" which Howells admired so warmly in the mature Tarkington and which gained him critical esteem as a "serious novelist." Although not unmarred by occasional lapses into melodrama and sentimentality, these works maintain a high level of objectivity in their turn of events and in the shaping of characters. Here, more than anywhere else in his writings, Tarkington devoted his considerable talent to subject matter worthy of his sharpest insight. In these products of his major phase, Tarkington merits appreciably more recognition as a perceptive witness of his time and place, as well as a talented craftsman in casting the social novel, than present-day judgment accords him.

## CHAPTER 5

# The Maker of Characters

A S Tarkington progressed from regional and historical romance to social criticism, his characters, like his objectives, assumed greater depth. Those characters which experienced the greatest amount of change were women, and their development gained Tarkington wide acclaim and elevated him to within the periphery of the modern school. For Tarkington to achieve such a status while still in his formative years was no small feat; for to titillate the feminine mystique at the turn of the century without offending its finer sensibilities took careful control. When he began writing, it was with all the Victorian reticence of his peers; but, through his fine craftsmanship, his acute awareness of the female readership, and his pursuit of "decorous realism," he swiftly developed the finesse in matters feminine which earned him new distinction.

## I *Women and the Writer's Market*

From all indications, female readers created major problems for Tarkington and his literary contemporaries, partly because of the economic implications of their massive readership and partly because of their prevailing image of inviolable womanhood. To begin with, popular magazines were rapidly becoming one of the most-read products of the media. Even seventy-five years ago, magazines had attained the status of big business; and, by the mid-1920's, Tarkington's peak period, Robert and Helen Lynd had noted in their classic study of Midland America that "today the Middletown Library offers 225 periodicals as against nineteen periodicals in 1890. Heavy, likewise, has been the increase in the number of magazines coming into Middle-town homes."[1]

To an adept Tarkington, an astute judge of both the literary mart and popular taste, the implications of this analysis could hardly have gone ignored. With the exception of *The Image of Josephine*, every Tarkington novel was first serialized in a periodical; and one of the most obvious limitations imposed by this kind of publication is the necessity of addressing an audience of fantastic diversity and dimensions.

That Tarkington was well aware of the preponderance of females among his readers is substantiated by his titles: *Alice Adams, Claire Ambler, Kate Fennigate, Women, The Flirt,* to cite but a few. And he knew, too, that the greatest number of these women were in their late teens or early twenties. William Dean Howells, in his critical essay "Realism and the American Novel" (1891), made this composition of the reading public very clear: "The novel in our American civilization now always addresses a mixed company, and the vast majority ... are ladies, and very many, if not most, ... are young girls."[2] Such persons, Tarkington himself observed, are avid novel readers "who seek to escape from life itself by the reading of romances." For women in general, he explained to Kenneth Roberts at the beginning of Roberts's career, "there must be a love affair with difficulties that always must be overcome in the end of the book." Older ladies in particular, he asserted, "love to repeat over and over vicariously in their reading the sensations of youthful love. Every woman ... wants a novel to repeat for her and let her live for a time in the repetition of the romantic dreams of love and a lover that she had in her youth before she knew the disappointing kind of things that may have happened to her."[3] We should remember, of course, that these are the remarks of an established author to a beginning writer. As such they are practical comments about the popular market which Roberts was seeking to enter, rather than the general readership which Tarkington aspired to reach in his peak years.

This feminine majority among novel readers raised another issue which persisted well into the twentieth century. As Tarkington realized, an intransigent image of WOMAN pervaded

every strata of American society in general and dominated
the editorial policies of magazines in particular. In *The Mauve
Decade*, a kaleidoscope of the United States in the 1890's,
Thomas Beer labels his opening section "The Titaness." Recog-
nizing the westward shift of the New England conscience, Beer
identifies the Titaness as that Middle Western woman who had
quietly become "a terror to editors, the hope of missionary
societies, and the prey of lecturers."[4] Although she was soon
to receive the full broadside of satire from Ring Lardner and
Sinclair Lewis, it is doubtful whether even that threat would
have deterred her. As a self-appointed censor of the entire
public domain of literature, she exerted an influence far beyond
reason. As Beer comments, "This is the period of which Frank
Stockton remarked that one letter of protest from some damned
nobody would raise more hell in a magazine's office than ten
letters of praise from intelligent people."[5] In *A Backward Glance*,
Edith Wharton expresses much the same sentiment (albeit
more politely) when she observes, "Again and again in my
literary life I have encountered the same kind of editorial
timidity." Later in the same volume she asserts, "The poor
novelists who were my contemporaries had to fight hard for
the right to turn wooden dolls about which they were sup-
posed to make believe into struggling, suffering human beings."[6]
In a classic bit of understatement, Beer concludes, "Young
writers of the '90s were aware that life and the notions of
editors clashed."

Although Tarkington was certainly aware of this forbidding
female figure which stalked the fields of fiction, he made little
effort to confront the Titaness and her editorial cohorts. Perhaps
as a native of the same Midwestern environment which had
bred "the Iron Virgin" (to borrow a phrase from Henry Adams),
he respected her power; more likely, as an aspiring novelist,
he yielded to her pronouncements out of sheer discretion.


## II  *The Early Heroines*

Although the course of Tarkington's feminine characterizations
cannot be neatly graphed, it is possible to trace a fairly distinct
order of development. At the far left stand the sweet young

things of the early, heavily plotted stories. Typical of these is Helen Sherwood, the "dainty little figure about five feet high" who graces the pages of *The Gentleman from Indiana*. Indeed, despite her modest dimensions, Helen set a pattern which Tarkington followed many times in subsequent novels: a demure young lady unobtrusively steers her beloved through a maze of complications to a happy resolution. In this well-paced novel, Helen's shrewd coverage of editorial duties during the recovery of John Harkless from an attack by the "Whitecaps" (ruffian counterparts of the Ku Klux Klan) keeps the Carlow *Herald* solvent and the political fortune of its editor hale while he is away from his desk. Likewise, Helen decoys the bemused young man farther and farther into "the tender trap," although she is careful not to spring it until the next to the last page.

Despite Tarkington's adroit manipulation of Helen in *The Gentleman from Indiana*, she remains little more than an attractive figure against a somewhat drab Hoosier landscape. The novelist provides her with ample descriptive detail, adequate dialogue, and a wide range of graphic actions; but he does so from the omniscient point of view typical of Tarkington's early works. In other words, the reader becomes familiar with Helen as a character in a novel, but he never knows her as a person. Then, too, there is a static quality about her—an absence of that organic growth so vital to verisimilitude in fiction. The Helen Sherwood whom John takes unto himself at the close of the romance is the same winsome girl he had met many pages earlier.

Soon after Helen Sherwood, we meet a piquant Ariel Tabor in *The Conquest of Canaan*, whose undertaking to resurrect a besotted Joe Louden (as well as directing a civic clean-up campaign at the same time) stretches our credulity. Sweet Mary Vertree of *The Turmoil* also holds shallow meaning for the reader. Indeed, nearly all of the youthful Tarkington's heroines are drawn from the same company; to the critic today, they are figments of an overcharged idealism. We may well agree with Robert Holliday, the pioneer biographer of Tarkington, that "most of the women in Mr. Tarkington's earlier books are not so much actual women as the embodiment of romantic and chivalrous dreams of women."[7]

### III   *La Femme fatale, à la Tarkington*

As early as 1907, a new breed of female came under the scrutiny of Tarkington. Although differing in detail within a variety of subspecies, the generic label is *la femme fatale*; but, as a stereotype, she belongs to a hardy breed which the reader accepts on faith. Whereas the Anglo-American novel includes the full genus, Tarkington provides but two varieties. The less significant of these is Continental, first represented by Madame Hélène de Veurigard in a novelette entitled *His Own People* (1907). In this overworked yarn about a nice American man gulled into gambling with foreign crooks, Madame de Veurigard first lures the "innocent abroad" into the snare set by her accomplices. Eventually she takes pity upon her victim; and the twist of the story consists of the clever ploy whereby she rescues the hapless American yet retains her role with her conspirators. Although Madame de Veurigard is the pivotal figure in a tale of intrigue, she is hardly a major character in a literary sense.

Cut from the same pattern is Madame Momoro, the *femme fatale* aboard the cruiseship *Duumvir* in Tarkington's novel *The Plutocrat,* written during the year following his last European junket in 1925. The svelte Mme. Momoro may enthrall the entire male passenger list aboard the *Duumvir*; but, to the reader, she too is but a cardboard figure of two dimensions. In this half-serious, half-hilarious work, her principal function is to reveal each man to be a knave upon a ship of fools. With obvious relish, Tarkington assembled on board all the victims of his literary spleen (each a member of some *avant-garde* school of letters) and then used the French seductress to expose their frailties. Hence *The Plutocrat* is more figurative than realistic, and Mme. Momoro too is not to be regarded as a genuine character study. In most respects, she is the "lady of mystery" so dear to the international romance; and Tarkington made no effort to add substance to her role.

But, if these French specimens are unimportant, the American versions of *la femme fatale* are neither simple conformists to a conventional stereotype nor stick figures on a puppet stage. Probably because Tarkington knew them so much better, the home products are also not copies from a prototype—each is an individual in her own right. Since this group comprise a goodly portion of Tarkington's gallery of women, it would be well to discuss a representative few of these fascinating figures.

The first of these, found in *The Flirt* (1913), is quite unlike the heroines of the sentimental romances; Cora Madison is a deliberate hypocrite who shapes every speech for a calculated effect and rehearses every move for a preconceived result. Obsessed with her own charm, she falls victim to shameless narcissism. With her fingertips she gently brushes her own lips; in her boudoir, she coquettes with herself before the mirror; at night, she cuddles herself to sleep on her own soft arms. Returning from a delicious evening with Valentine Corliss, the villain of the piece, she pensively relives the earlier hours as she sits before her dressing-table. Suddenly, suffused with memories, "she leaned very closely, closer and yet closer to the mirror; a rich colour spread over her; her eyes, gazing into themselves, became dreamy, inexpressibly wistful, cloudily sweet, her breath was tumultuous. . . . Then, in the final moment, as her face almost touched the glass, she forgot how and what she looked to Corliss; she forgot him utterly: she leaped to her feet and kissed the mirrored lips with passion. 'You darling!' she cried." With the most un-Freudian candor, Tarkington adds: "Cora's christening had been unimaginative, for the name means only 'maiden.' She should have been called Narcissa."[8]

A clue exists in this casual comment by the author; for, by extension, the simple word "christening" suggests that Cora Madison grew into her role as she matured in years. At this pre-Amberson stage, however, the artistry of Tarkington was unequal to the demands which the coquette imposed as a serious study. Unlike Sinclair Lewis, for example, Tarkington rarely attacked the complexities of tracing his central characters from youth into maturity. Thus the reader meets Cora Madison in *The Flirt* at the peak of her sexuality, and he leaves her only a few months later. Despite the sensational theatricalism which vitiates the novel itself, the reader must agree with Arthur Quinn that "Cora Madison is the first of those remarkable pictures of women which have elicited the admiration and even wonder of their own sex at Tarkington's insight."[9]

In many respects, she is Tarkington's most successful characterization up to this point in his career. Woodress remarks of
Cora, "She is a terrifying beauty who actually is a far greater
menace than the confidence man Corliss. Irresponsible, thought-
less, self-centered, she embroils her father and her fiancé in
Corliss' schemes, blights her older sister's life, and then con-
temptuously dismisses Corliss." Significantly, he concludes, "Cora
is the *femme fatale* of literary history, a kindred spirit, certainly,
with Circe, Becky Sharp, and Sister Carrie, and one of many
such Tarkington ladies."[10]

Despite the popularity of *The Flirt*, Tarkington did not immediately follow his portraiture of Cora Madison with variations
on her pattern. Instead, he turned back the calendar to Marjorie
Jones, the subteen, flaxen-haired charmer in a juvenile *Penrod*
(1913), then up a bit to Miss Pratt, the late-teen mistress of
baby-talk in an adolescent *Seventeen* (1915). Each of these
creatures is wise beyond her years to the ways of males, each
is unusually aware of the wiles of women, but both are only
the light characters of juvenile fiction. Even Julia Atwater, the
ineffably lovely heroine of *Gentle Julia* (1922), has become
by that time just another "sweet young thing" in a porch-swing
romance. For Tarkington, now entering his major phase, the old
stereotype of the *femme fatale* had obviously lost its appeal.

## IV  The Complete Woman

With the publication of *Alice Adams* (1921), Tarkington
began a completely new direction in his feminine studies.
Although traces of *The Flirt* persist, this chronicle of a young
woman's efforts to mount the social ladder in small-town
America conveys a genuine sense of honest reality. The daughter
of a hapless glue manufacturer, Alice is determined to rise
above her sordid situation by every means at her disposal.
Without the support of friends, without the resources of family,
and without principle or propriety, she lays siege to Arthur
Russell, the most eligible bachelor at the moment. To the
dismay of inveterate consumers of romance, she fails; and
the novel closes when Alice confronts "that dark entrance to
the wooden stairway leading up to Frincke's Business College—

the very doorway she had always looked upon as the end of youth and the end of hope."[11]

Tarkington had misgivings about the novel, for he questioned whether his readers would become interested in has-beens like the Adamses. After all, he reasoned, these are pretty ordinary folks caught up in pretty ordinary affairs. In his quest for realism, he feared just what the reviewer for the *Literary Digest* reported about *Alice Adams*: "The author has succumbed to the craze for detail to the great detriment of his work, and just in so far as he is photographic he is dull. The conversations between Alice and Russell may be literally true, but they are inexcusable in a work of fiction. For the first time Mr. Tarkington is occasionally tiresome."[12] In contrast, fellow novelist Ellen Glasgow, who shared many of Tarkington's literary ideals, wrote him in admiration of *Alice Adams*: "You have achieved two things that I had believed almost impossible in American fiction; you have written of average people without becoming an average writer and you have treated the American girl without sentimentality. The end of the story is very fine and true— and it makes absolutely no concession to the ubiquitous devourer of the second rate."[13] Sinclair Lewis as well, who was sweeping the country on a lecture tour in the wake of *Main Street* (1920), reported to Tarkington that everywhere he was telling his audience, "When you are considering the clever unknown youngsters, don't ever suppose that because he sells so enormously, Booth Tarkington can't write better than any of them."[14]

Such words of praise from Tarkington's peers were more than matched by other accolades that followed. Not only did he receive the Pulitzer Prize for *Alice Adams* but also honorary degrees were showered upon him by Princeton, his alma mater; by Columbia University; and by DePauw University, his father's school. At the same time that he was achieving academic recognition, he began winning popularity polls conducted by various publications. In 1921, when *Publisher's Weekly* asked bookmen to name "the most significant contemporary American authors," Tarkington led a long list. In the following year, when the *Literary Digest* made a similar survey, Tarkington was voted "the greatest living American author"; in a *New York Times* contest, he was the only writer named in a list of "the ten greatest contemporary Americans." To his credit, it must be added that he wore these honors lightly; in fact, they were an embarrassment to him more often than a distinction. (After 1924, he made it a policy not to accept additional honorary degrees. Only Purdue University succeeded in slipping one more hood over his shoulders at a special ceremony at his home in Indianapolis in 1940.)

The reasons for the overwhelming approval of *Alice Adams* are not hard to find. Written in the summer seclusion of Kennebunkport, the novel reflects careful forethought and planning in the artistic control evident in every aspect of its realistic manner. Originally, the novelist had conceived it as the third volume of *Growth,* but the heroine of the story had other ideas. As a consequence of her intransigence, Tarkington postponed his observations on Midwestern history until *The Midlander* and permitted *Alice Adams* to emerge as a separate study of an individual rather than as one of a family; but the novel is not merely a character study of a covetous young woman. It probes deeply into the materialism which Tarkington regarded as rampant in 1920; it exposes the corrosive effects of the money mania which beset the Adams family; and it dramatizes the destruction wrought by the family's senseless drive for social position. The core of the novel, however, is Alice.

Alice Adams is Tarkington's most nearly complete woman. Despite frequent susceptibility to the charms of his other creations, Tarkington managed to maintain an objectivity toward Alice which allowed her an unusual degree of freedom. Her story represents Tarkington's prime example of what he called "the investigatory novel." This expression, like the "intensivism" of Howells and "veritism" of Garland, has remained well on the periphery of critical terminology, yet it does have its utility. In brief, Tarkington presented this type of novel as a work of fiction "intended to investigate human beings and if possible to reveal something about them."[15] To be effective, therefore, the characters had to be drawn as closely as possible from life in order that they might possess a convincing realism which the reader could accept without hesitation. In other words, the verity of a novel is in direct proportion to the authenticity of the characters and their actions.

In the Tarkington sense of the word, "investigatory" should not imply either the reportorial technique or the mechanistic impersonalization of the Naturalist school. Both of these approaches implied a dehumanization of subject matter which was anathema to his artistic principles. For him, the term "investigatory" means merely the author's acceptance of his characters as real people. Once they acquire substance, they must be permitted free range in their thoughts, actions, and speech. Regardless of consequences, they must be allowed to make mistakes, to go astray, to fail. Above all, Tarkington declared in 1945, the figures in a novel "mustn't fall into fiction patterns. What they feel, think, and do mustn't conform to the literary expectations of the reader more accommodatingly than do the actual creatures of flesh about him."[16]

Tarkington's thesis that the worthiest novel is an investigation of human beings who approximate real people creates its own problem. He was by no means so naïve as to conceive of human personality as a simple, transparent subject. Indeed, he wrote that, "If for some moments the reader will think hard of his circle of friends and acquaintances, he'll perceive that his thoughts are really roving among strangers."[17] How much more difficult, then, the creative process becomes when an author seeks to breathe life into "the airy nothings" of his own imagination. In the opinion of Tarkington, the synthesis of personality in fiction is an intricate process demanding not only keen observation and a retentive memory, but also a vivid imagination which has a full view of one's creation and the discrimination to select the contributive details.

Thus, Alice Adams achieves reality because throughout her creation, Tarkington occupied that *locus operandi* from which he could best observe her under all circumstances but could exert over her only those minimal controls required by the form of the novel. As a recognizable human being, Alice is a complicated character. The mature Tarkington sensed that the more obvious, the more simple, the more consistent the persons portrayed are, the less real they appear: "If the people in the book are to 'come alive' to the eye and ear of an observant reader, those people must not be easier to know all about than actual people."[18] Through the pages of *Alice Adams*, the reader may well find his attitude toward the heroine shifting from pity to scorn, from sympathy to disgust, and perhaps at last from aversion to admiration. To Tarkington, this change of heart betokens the success of the novelist; for his studied opinion was that the characters in a novel "must be people about whom the reader could change his opinion, as he does sometimes, of real people; and his likes and dislikes may alter accordingly. The people of a book, to seem human, must be as inconsistent, for instance, as human beings are, and must inspire in one another as diverse opinions of themselves as all human beings do."[19]

It is a credit to Tarkington that Alice is a true charmer, despite her vanity, pretension, and histrionics. Although fully aware of Alice's selfish motive, the reader has to admire her determination to escape from an impossible family situation. Watching her range the park to gather violets for her own corsage, put on her "lost partner" act at Mildred Palmer's dancing party, and mount the dingy steps to Frincke's Business College at the close of the tale, the reader almost forgets the family strife she has created with her demands for money, social position, and marital security. He almost overlooks her cheap flirtations, her flagrant falsehoods, and her deliberate deceptions in the summer romance with Arthur Russell.

To the majority of critics, *Alice Adams* constitutes Tarkington's supreme accomplishment in the art of storytelling. Carl Van Doren explains why: "In the career of Alice Adams [Tarkington] kept his conscience honest to the last and has produced a masterpiece."[20] That is to say, in this novel Tarkington created a reprehensible character who ultimately gets exactly what she deserves. Despite her basic integrity (symbolized by the upward climb into the sunlight in the closing scene), and despite the author's latent partiality, all her dreams are blasted. As a consequence, wrote Edith Wyatt in the *North American Review* soon after the novel emerged, "In the mid-western scene which Mr. Tarkington presents to us so admirably, Alice Adams herself, what she is, what spiritual materials she has for making her life, become known to us with a pathos, a reality and subtlety that belong to the last excellence of craftsmanship."[21]

Although Alice Adams may be Tarkington's finest female figure, she by no means climaxed his interest in feminine

character. Indeed, the many who followed her—his egotistical
flirts, shrewish vixens, and calculating schemers—hold an undeniably greater appeal than do their prim and proper sisters;
and we meet such a *mélange* in *Women* (1925), a composite
study of those types of womankind at which Tarkington
excelled. In Arthur Quinn's perceptive work, *American Fiction:
An Historical and Critical Survey*, Quinn comments that "In
*Women* Tarkington's uncanny knowledge of feminine nature
is revealed more than once. In particular the devices by which
a young woman takes a man away from a much finer rival
are almost blood-curdling in their realism."[22] Writing for *The
Bookman* in 1927, no doubt with *Women* in mind, Joseph
Collins confirmed Quinn's opinion: "There is no denying that
he learned women's minds from keen observation, and he knows
how to make them stand out in a background of familiar environment. His women act, talk, think, and suffer much as women
do in real life, they have hysterics and sharp tongues like real
women, and they are done with the fine end of a pen dipped in
subtle ink. By going from one house to another, raising roofs
and looking in, Mr. Tarkington has done a gallery of feminine
pictures which reveal him as a serious student and a painter
of character."[23]

Only three years after *Women*, Tarkington introduced in
*Claire Ambler* (1928) still another of those huntresses who
lead sham lives of selfish pretense only to fall victims to the
tragedy which comes with the realization of their self-deception.
For the most part, this tale is a modernized version of the
international novel made popular by fellow genteel Realists
like Henry James in *Daisy Miller* (1878) and William Dean
Howells in *A Fearful Responsibility* (1881). An inveterate
flirt, Claire is introduced in America as a flighty debutante of
eighteen at a vacation spot reminiscent of Kennebunkport.
Appearing next in Raona, Sicily, Claire soon captivates a goodly
following of young Italians; but she devotes her principal
attention to a dying British war veteran. Claire passes unscathed
from affair to affair, shielded by her American innocence. Only
after she discovers that, inadvertently, her "fast and loose" behavior away from home nearly brings about the death of one
Italian admirer does she realize her true nature. "No wonder I do

such harm!" she thought. "My very soul is artificial—and hideous!"[24] Although marred by moments of melodrama, *Claire Ambler,* like *The Flirt,* remains an intriguing study of narcissism and its destructive consequences.

One final example serves to indicate the perennial interest of this theme for Tarkington. Even as late as 1943, only three years before his death, he depicted another enchantress as the counterpart for Kate Fennigate in the novel which bears her name. Invited by the *Saturday Evening Post* to "write a story about a woman who is responsible for her husband's business," Tarkington took his concept of a twentieth-century heroine *in toto* from a seventeenth-century portrait on his study wall. In *Some Old Portraits* he had written of the subject in the painting: "She's a woman natively gifted with the talent we call executive ability; and she knows she has it and her use of it is intuitive."[25] Kate Fennigate is portrayed in precisely the same terms.

As foil for Kate, the competent heroine of the novel, Tarkington introduced Laila Capper, a domineering woman whose influence is invariably disruptive or evil. In contrast to the wholesome Kate, Laila is a cheap, conniving female. By the age of fifteen the precocious girl had become aware of men and of her attractiveness to them. Soon she also had her philosophy of marriage: "Oh, I'll not be in any hurry to marry. I'm going to have lots and lots of fun first, and afterwards too if I want to, because that's really the only way clever women get their share out of this life. I'm going to be a bird in a gilded cage; but the cage isn't going to have any top on it."[26] Laila Capper's determination to pursue this creed motivates a good part of the activity in this vigorous novel— as well as Tarkington's most suggestive lines. Although her machinations work tragedy in the lives of all she affects, her *coup de grâce* is deflected so skillfully by Kate that Laila is cut low by her own misdeeds. Such a philosophy of retribution is a familiar pattern within the Tarkington novels already discussed, particularly in *The Flirt* and in *Claire Ambler*; it also operates in lesser sketches of women of the workaday world, like *Young Mrs. Greeley* and *The Lorenzo Bunch.*

Although critic Hjalmar Boyesen made the following remark,

novelist Booth Tarkington should have done so: "I have always
sympathized with the perverter of Pope who declared that the
noblest study of mankind is woman; and of all womankind
no variety better repays sympathetic and discriminating study
than the American."[27] Although none of Tarkington's feminine
studies following *Alice Adams* elevated his status in this fictional
field, few diminished it. Indeed, each portrait depicts in its
own way the perennial interest which women held for him.
As Henry James is said to have done, Tarkington looked at
women rather as women look at them; women look at women
as persons, men look at them as women. This ability stood him
in good stead across four decades of a full career.

### V  *The Incomplete Man*

These comments about female characters should not be
interpreted as implying that Tarkington was mainly a ladies'
man. As fellow Hoosier R. E. Banta observed in an early article,
"Tarkington has been happy in his choice of male associates
throughout his life."[28] In fact, a whole chapter could easily
be constructed from the testimonials of affectionate esteem
from men of every walk of life. When Carl D. Bennett, the
early academic critic of Tarkington, spent one summer on a
Carnegie grant doing field work among former Tarkington associates, nothing struck him more than the broad popularity
of the man. "Everywhere," Bennett reported, "at Princeton
University, in Maine, at Phillips Exeter Academy, at Purdue
University, and particularly in Indianapolis, the name of Booth
Tarkington was *open sesame*."[29] Much the same observation
was made by Woodress after examining the Tarkington Papers
at Princeton: "Tarkington's interests were broad, his friends
varied; and his letters went to writers, artists, statesmen, and
businessmen, who discussed with him everything from old paintings to the atomic bomb."[30] Not only did Tarkington make
new friends easily, but he kept the old ones. Every indication
points to his possessing an ingratiating personality which en-
deared him to a host of admirers, male and female alike.

On the other hand, the silence among critics regarding Tarkington's male creations is indicative of an inescapable fact:

whereas he excelled in his portraits of women, many of his men are quite ordinary daubs. They are neither glaringly deficient in execution nor conspicuously successful. Recalling Tarkington's galaxy of masculine friends, we are at a loss to explain this hiatus in his achievements. Certainly, opportunity was never lacking for the analytical observation of many kinds of men in most kinds of circumstances. Yet not one of his adult males can stand beside a bristling handful from the pen of Sinclair Lewis (whose feminine characters are often correspondingly weak). Numerically speaking, a good third of Tarkington's novels appear to be man-centered, but the statistics are misleading. Even a superficial survey reveals that these works are not personality studies in the deeper sense of the term as much as they are various fictional types of male characters.

In the first place, certainly no one would defend as character studies the heroes of regional romances like *The Gentleman from Indiana* or *The Conquest of Canaan*. In the former, John Harkless of the *Herald* is as unabashedly an idealized a hero as Helen Sherwood, the heroine—nor does one detect the least sign of organic growth in him as the plot unrolls. The young man who steps off the train at Plattville at the close of the novel is quite the same person who descended the same steps in the first chapter. Similarly, the youthful Joe Louden of *The Conquest of Canaan* is buffeted about by fitful gusts of melodrama. However, he too conquers in the end, embracing simultaneously a blushing Ariel Tabor and the same virtues which drew him back to a home town determined to deny him. The idealistic theme of dedicated altruism so dominates every aspect of both novels that character growth is impossible.

A second variety of Tarkington's tales likewise offers little potentiality for significant characterization, for rarely does the author of historical romance weave a substantial study of personality within the fabric of his story. The figures in such novels are stereotyped by convention, and the heightened action is designed to capitalize on the ready-built virtues of heroic types. Thus *Monsieur Beaucaire*, exquisite though it may be in stylistic artistry, remains sheer romance. The gallant Frenchman doffs his role as "Monsieur le Duc de Chateaurien" when the masquerade is over; he has played his part with supreme *élan*, but it is only a part. At his exit, he is quite the same blade we met at his entrance. And in *Cherry*, as Joseph Collins noted, "not attempting to describe life as it is, or as it should be, he [Tarkington] simply relates a dream, in the Beaucaire manner, with a smile in his pen and a song in his heart."[31] In reality, *Cherry* is pure pastiche, a rare work of comic restraint, but one far removed from sober character analysis. One anonymous reviewer of *Wanton Mally* (1932), Tarkington's belated return to this genre, was so lost for terms for the work that he opened his remarks by calling it "a novel rather than a romance," then concluded by labeling it a "fable." Like the rest of Tarkington's historical fabrications, it can hardly be ranked as a psychological study on any level.

In Tarkington's more contemporary romances, the male characterization is better, but the harvest is still meager. *The Two Vanrevels* (vaguely mid-nineteenth century) is an inconsequential fantasy based on the worn mistaken-identity device. Amid the heavy atmosphere of suspense around a mysterious figure, there is little opportunity for character analysis; the plot is the essential feature. A later novel remotely akin to *The Two Vanrevels* is *The Guest of Quesnay,* a psychologized account of an amnesiac that is reminiscent of *Random Harvest* by James Hilton. In theme, *The Guest of Quesnay* is a fictionalization of the *tabula rasa* theory propounded by John Locke. The magnitude of the plan, complicated even further by undefined religious motifs, is never fulfilled; the work remains a plot-heavy novel of limited analytical depth which descends eventually into pure melodrama.

For a fourth group of characters, we should investigate the realm of the lighter fiction with a humorous cast at which Tarkington was such a master; for there we find a collection of rogues who constitute some of his most amusing contributions to literary entertainment. The novels in this category, however, are even less rewarding in significant character portrayal than the earlier ones. In terms of what Tarkington called "the investigatory novel," none of these approaches the status of permanent letters. It is indicative of their superficial nature that these are all episodic works centered upon lovable eccentrics caught within the maze of typical situation comedies. In this category, we should place such works as *The Rumbin Galleries*, an engaging sketch of a wily art dealer; *The Fighting Littles*, with its not-quite-profane "job-jamming" father; and *Mary's Neck* (a geographical reference, by the way), with its long-suffering Mr. Massey, his antique-loving wife, and their two boy-crazy daughters. Each of these novels makes delightful reading, but it would be folly to describe them as anything more than entertainment.

## VI  *The Figurative Man*

For quite different reasons, we also cannot consider other males of a seriocomic nature. The motley passenger list of the *Duumvir* in *The Plutocrat* provides a case in point. For a conservative Tarkington, each of the *artistes* aboard personifies, as we have observed, some branch of decadent "modern art." In particular, we soon meet an unholy trinity: Ogle, the "sophisticated" author of a cynical risqué comedy; Machlyn, the *avant garde* poet who "tries to make people notice him by using no punctuation and omitting capital letters"; and Jones, the unsung modernistic artist who "creates for the few." Though Tarkington tells his tale with high good humor, it is obvious to the reader that all such characters are only straw figures set up by Tarkington to pierce with barbs of sharp satire. In a burlesque like *The Plutocrat*, we must accept the flatness of caricature; and it is idle to lament with critic Lawrence Morris that "neither Ogle [the playwright in the novel] nor the plutocrat ever becomes a three-dimensional individual."

For all of Earl Tinker's simplicity, he posed peculiar problems for Tarkington. Like virtually every American novelist intrigued by the successful businessman, "Tarkington seems to have been greatly attracted to men of power, but to have doubted all the time the propriety of such an attraction."[32] By the conclusion of *The Plutocrat*, however, "the New Roman" emerges as victor over all the intellectual and artistic forces arrayed before him: "For, in the cloud of dust against the sun, the powerful and humorous figure, still standing and waving as it rode on toward long-conquered Carthage, seemed to have become gigantic."[33] To Michael Millgate, writing in *American*

*Social Fiction* (1964), "this is the apotheosis of the businessman in the American novel." Quite properly, however, Millgate too remains disturbed by the plutocrat; indeed, in his final judgment, Millgate declares that "Tarkington, taking more and more the side of the businessman, eventually makes Earl Tinker a lord of the earth without for a moment making him an attractive or even a credible human being."[34]

There can be no doubt that this ambiguity in the final function of the plutocrat arises from a persistent conflict between Tarkington's intentions as a social critic and the intransigence of his material. Deeply rooted in the literary idealism and social decorum of the genteel tradition, yet stirred by the drama of Growth and Big Business, he sought throughout his life some happy solution to this perplexing dichotomy between esthetics and economics. In *The Plutocrat*, this uncertainty results in a Tinker who alternates between compassion and insensitivity, between courage and compromise, between genius and philistinism. Sensing the inadequacy of his own offspring, Tarkington sets up an incredible match between Olivia, the lissome daughter of Tinker, and Laurence Ogle, the playwright, in the hope that this marriage of means and minds may result in a new generation that will incorporate the best of both worlds.

## VII  *The Symbolic Man*

Even in the *Growth* trilogy, with all its power and promise, we might raise questions about at least two of the "heroes." As noted earlier, from Howells to the present, Bibbs Sheridan of *The Turmoil* (1915) has been construed as a sorry sacrifice of Art to Mammon. About the second study in the series, *The Midlander* (1923), Michael Millgate writes, "The hero . . . is undoubtedly Dan Oliphant, the forceful businessman and speculative builder, but we see him always from a distance. . . . Consequently as a character Dan himself scarcely exists."[35] Such a stricture, however, evades the dynamic force of Dan as an entrepreneur in generating the thematic significance of this powerful novel. Handicapped as a young man fresh out of college with no working capital, no family support, and no backing from investors, "Dan ultimately becomes the general promoter of the city's growth, the founder of an automobile manufacturing company, a dabbler in interurban lines, and Mayor for a term."[36]

Although *The Midlander* closes on a clear note of hope, much of the novel is somber in tone; and Dan is certainly a low-key hero. In Tarkington's determination to keep the work as realistic as possible, he depicted the setting in all the bleakness of a city in travail, replete with ugliness and dirt, greed and corruption. Himself the victim of change, Dan dies of pneumonia amid the throes of marital distress and financial failure. Like Bibbs Sheridan, however, Dan Oliphant is not a tragic figure; he exists largely as a symbol of the unavoidable compromise which must accompany the "practical idealism" which underlies so much of Tarkington's social philosophy.

Although similarities exist between Bibbs Sheridan of *The Turmoil* and Dan Oliphant of *The Midlander*, striking differences also appear. Because Tarkington is a better craftsman ten years later, Dan emerges in far greater depth, in much fuller dimension. The reader meets Bibbs as a college graduate, and he leaves him not many years later. Dan, on the other hand, is introduced as an "all-boy" youngster, carried along as a collegian who graduates "not altogether without difficulty," and left as an adult who "would prefer a concert by Sousa's Band" to a symphony program. In other words, there is a development in Dan Oliphant which we do not find in Bibbs Sheridan. Although Dan's youthful "boosting" is not unlike "the brag" of Earl Tinker in *The Plutocrat*, he becomes a sober, hardworking citizen who accepts the responsibilities of maturity. Even in his marriage to a vixen from the East, he keeps to the end his part of a poor bargain. Symbol though he remains, this protagonist of *The Midlander* comes close to full manhood.

*The Magnificent Ambersons* is not only the first novel for which Tarkington won the Pulitzer Prize; it is also the work in which we meet Tarkington's most memorable male. To some extent, no doubt, George Minafer borrows his stature from *The Magnificent Ambersons* itself, for this rangy novel embraces three generations. Within its commodious pages, little Georgie, the last scion of the Amberson stock, has room to grow from infancy to manhood and time to undergo that sea change which transforms him from an incorrigible brat to a humble suitor. Upon this last point critics tend to split; some suggest that Tarkington himself did not realize "how really horrid George is"; hence, it is "too difficult" for readers to accept his reformation at the end. Others feel that George does not "suffer enough" to learn the compassion he ultimately displays. Perhaps most important, a considerable contingent decries the fitness of the "happy ending" for such an insufferable snob. In this instance, for a discerning woman like Lucy Morgan to take back an absolute heel like George Minafer may be too great a stretch for the reader's credulity.

Perhaps Tarkington wrought better than he knew, for George is an unheroic hero. Again and again he demonstrates that he is an arrogant egotist. We watch him pursue from infancy an ever lonelier path because of his self-righteous air and his high-handed behavior. When he dismisses Lucy's father as his mother's suitor, we are appalled by his duplicity; when he spurns Lucy's open love, we are shocked by his cruelty. Inexorably, however, the tide of fortune changes. In utter helplessness he sees the Amberson dynasty crumble about him until he is left bankrupt and alone.

To many critics, that is precisely how a George Minafer should be left. When accused of partiality, Tarkington replied mildly that "he wrote what he wrote because that was the way he had to." In *The Turmoil*, Bibbs Sheridan adjusts to the exigencies of his dilemma; in *The Midlander*, Dan Oliphant succumbs upon the very brink of success; in *Alice Adams*, three years later, Alice loses her matrimonial campaign; in *The Magnificent Ambersons*, George Minafer rises from near annihilation to a future of hope. For the final figure of the *Growth* trilogy, there was no other way for George to go. In this novel of broad social change, he must remain as the pivotal figure between a benighted past and an enlightened future.

Regardless of our attitude toward the outcome of *The Magnificent Ambersons*, we cannot remain unmoved by it. Enforced by solid subject matter and substantial theme, George Minafer invades the memory. In this novel, Tarkington provides a worthy proving-ground on which to test the mettle of his protagonist. Like the author himself, George passes through a critical period in recent American history, and he finds it an excruciating experience. Despite the pangs of change, however, George not only survives but matures. Alongside the theme of socio-economic growth which unifies the trilogy, there runs a complementary theme of growth in George. Woven together most tightly in *The Magnificent Ambersons*, the two themes make for a moving study of a man and his times.

## VIII  *The Role of Character*

It is no coincidence that each Tarkington masterpiece of characterization is the protagonist of a prize-winning novel. What one must realize, however, is that the woman and the man come into being for different reasons. Alice Adams becomes the heroic figure she is because of her indomitable drive for the full life as she conceives it. Stripped to naked shame by her own machinations, Alice is left alone to salvage what fragments she can. Yet, she climbs upward, step by step, heartened only by a shaft of sunlight from a distant window. For once, Tarkington is little help to his foster child—and she grows from neglect. Unlike many of his heroines, Alice Adams leaps from the page a living woman—conniving and predatory, true, yet evoking a compassion reserved for her alone among Tarkington's women.

On the other hand, the fidelity of George Minafer is diminished somewhat by his reversal in character at the close of *The Magnificent Ambersons*. George gains his stature more by his function as symbol than by his role as a person. When the fame and fortune of his family pass, he slips into an anonymity which only calamity can dispel. By that time his identity as a viable individual has become subordinated to his use as a mediary of past gentility in its union, through Lucy, with emergent mercantilism. Though the reader may not soon forget young Georgie, the incorrigible youngster, he easily permits George Minafer, the grown man, to merge into symbol as the book draws to a somewhat abrupt close.

In more general terms, we cannot overstress the abiding importance of characterization in all Tarkington writings of consequence. Throughout four decades of active publication, he maintained an absorbing interest in "the people" whom he met. Much like Charles Dickens in this respect, Tarkington combined an encyclopedic memory and a fertile imagination to create a wide assortment of memorable personalities. These defy categorization, for Tarkington ranged at will across various age levels, among several ethnic groups, and within different socio-economic classes. At times he might drop the thread of his narrative or lose sight of his objective, but Tarkington rarely mislaid his characters. To the author and his readers alike, they were his most precious commodity.

## CHAPTER 6

# The Juvenile World

N O critical study of Booth Tarkington would be complete without a review of the special contribution he made to American juvenile literature. As a matter of fact, for the adult reader today who recalls his own youth, Tarkington remains the author of "those Penrod stories" and, probably, of *Seventeen*. There is a bittersweet aspect to this identification since Tarkington, the mature artist, cherished the expectation that whatever literary immortality he achieved might come from his studies of the shifting adult world about him. In the course of time, this hope may well be realized; the Penrod days of pre-World War I are long gone, and the reading taste of two new generations of youngsters has changed drastically over succeeding years. "A boy's doings in the days when the stable was empty but not yet rebuilt into a garage," as Tarkington described *Penrod*, will surely seem more and more remote as the "hot-rod" set gets ever younger. Contrariwise, the social history bred into the *Growth* trilogy, into *Alice Adams*, and into Depression studies like "This Boy Joe" and *The Heritage of Hatcher Ide* will just as surely preserve them as pages of the American record long after more youthful fare has been forgotten.

To complicate matters, Tarkington himself regarded his juvenile writings in somewhat contradictory ways. Especially in the earlier years, he tended to look upon this type of fiction as primarily pleasant relaxation for himself and as the happy re-creation of youth for his readers. There is no question that he greatly enjoyed recapturing those childhood escapades hidden in the recesses of his memory. With reference to *Penrod*, James Woodress remarks, "An abundance of usable material was stored

101

up within him, and all he needed was the time and the place for concentrated effort and something to precipitate his experience."[1] Indeed, in many respects, Tarkington had been preparing all his life to write his juvenile tales. "I know what makes Penrod," Tarkington wrote of his most notorious youngster, "because I've been years on the job."[2] As has been noted heretofore, most of his childhood was a pleasant period for young Tark; consequently, his stories about children are rich in nostalgia, warm in tone, bright in color. More often than not, his writing on this level ranges from the light to the humorous to the hilarious—and back again.

## I  *The Hazardous Path to Adulthood*

On the other hand, an aging Tarkington found more and more to be sober about concerning these formative years. Contrary to many a critic, Tarkington held no illusions about this stage in life. "Childhood is not the Golden Age," he declared in *Looking Forward*; "happiness is unmitigated and flawless while it lasts, but so is grief."[3] As he regarded childhood, he thought it a treacherous time of disillusionment and false security. "Bright-browed youth has the illusion that it lives among certainties seeing solids all round about it," he commented in his unfinished autobiography, *As I Seem to Me*; "whereas it's like a complacent cocooned creature blown from its twig and unaware that it's being tossed vagrantly through underbrush in the dark."[4] Although not so bleak in his pessimism as this brief observation may suggest, Tarkington did become increasingly aware of the growing complexities besetting youth in mid-century America.

In reference to Tarkington's early juvenile writings, he spoke most about the awkward age when the chrysalis emerges from the cocoon. Protected by the infinite filaments of family love, the child has created a wish-world for himself in which he is quite innocent of the harsh and the unpleasant. Awakening to stern realities can be an excruciating experience; indeed, to Tarkington, it often constitutes one of the major tragedies of youth. "The child," he said, "lives almost as much in his dreams of what will happen as the very aged man does in his dream of

what has happened.... Moreover, there are sharper pains for
the child in his period of adjustment for life—and the child
has less ability to bear pain."[5] This theme, found especially in
the antics of Willie Baxter in *Seventeen,* is implicit in all
Tarkington's studies of the transition from childhood to young
adulthood.

Much of this tragicomedy of youth comes from the impasse
which develops between parents and their children: age has
forgotten the anguish of youth; youth knows nothing of age. In
some hands, this thesis could lead to the very depths of tragedy,
but Tarkington chose to take the upward path. Impelled in
part by the genteel realism of Howells but motivated more by
his own inner optimism and good breeding, Tarkington resorts
most often to the shafts of satire and the barbs of wit when
dealing with the seriocomic conflicts of youth and age (more
properly, youngster and parents). Not infrequently, the humor
derived from these juvenile dilemmas is largely an adult re-
action; to the young folk, victimized by a world not of their
making, these same situations are far from funny. In fact, were
it not for Tarkington's careful control over exaggeration, not
a few situations might remain pathetically serious.

In his maturity, Tarkington laid down another dictum which
may aid in clarifying the perennial appeal which these stories
of childhood through adolescence held for him. In an *American
Magazine* article, "What I Learned from Boys" (1925), Tarkington explained: "I began to see that, just as in his embryo man
reproduces the history of his development from the mire into
man, so does he in his childhood and his boyhood and his youth
reproduce the onward history of his race, from the most ancient
man to the most modern."[6] In other words, the child in his
microcosm relives the entire story of mankind in his growth
from infancy to adulthood. Like the story of Genesis, this may
best be interpreted in figurative rather than literal terms: men
in general undergo a sequence of experiences which have at
their inception those same drives which motivated primeval
man—ones which persist to this day. Through this allegorical
explanation, Tarkington was able to account for infantile selfishness, for childish cruelty, for adolescent passions.

In this respect, he found the "Penrod period" particularly

revealing. As he expressed it, "From eight to fourteen is a period of life piquantly interesting to the congenial observer; for in studying it he may perceive unconcealed in the boy not only what is later to be found coated over in the man but something also of the history of all mankind."[7] During these formative years, the child dashes through almost the full gamut of emotions and muddles through a wide variety of social experiences. In the process, Tarkington found the juvenile catalogue of drives and desires only too complete. Indeed, even after excluding those which he deemed improper for fictional purposes, there was no dearth of material.

Tarkington's concept of barbaric youth was tempered with a genial insistence that such primitivism is a quite normal stage in the evolution from infant to adult. With typical whimsy, he twitted the contemporary school of child psychology which proclaimed that "man is natively criminal." In mock gratitude, he asserted the convenience of this discovery, since "here we have expert opinion agreeing with the ancient lament, 'We are all miserable sinners'; and with many a badgered spinster's complaint that there never was a boy who didn't have the Old Harry in him."[8] And, indeed, among Tarkington's own juvenile characters, there are few cherubim.

Throughout Tarkington's juvenile works, his custom is to toss in frequent psychological tidbits. Carl Van Doren regards these with a somewhat jaundiced eye: "The knowing asides which accompany these juvenile records have been mistaken too often for shrewd, even for profound, analyses of human nature. Actually they are only knowing, as sophomores are knowing with respect to their juniors by a few years."[9] Van Doren's attitude represents, however, a minority report; the preponderance of critics have taken the opposite viewpoint in their acclaim for Tarkington as a unique artist in his ability to recapture those quirks of youth which age remembers only when prompted. Fred Lewis Pattee, for example, avers that Tarkington's " 'little monsters' are the amusing, spontaneous, and genuine creations of one who knew both the humor and the tragedy of adolescence in a mainstreet Western town."[10] Even Grant C. Knight, a reluctant admirer, admits that "in one respect at least Mr. Tarkington excells. His portraits of adolescent boys and girls are inimitable. It is true that they contain not a little exaggeration, but they are essentially right."[11] The overwhelming popularity of Tarkington's juvenile writings among the general public is also an indication of considerable agreement with his pronouncements of homespun child psychology which often have a folksy, epigrammatic style that gives them a specious authenticity which deters judicious analysis. Moreover, there is frequently a gently chiding quality, "maturity forgets that once . . ." or "the grown man has lost . . .," which discourages critical judgment, lest the judge himself be accused.

These side remarks by Tarkington assume added significance as a graver novelist is borne by the sullen current of the Depression into the turbulence of World War II. The didacticism swings more and more from the personal and the psychological toward the general and the sociological. As his career drew to a close, Tarkington became increasingly convinced of the constructive forces of fiction in a world bent on destruction. Sometimes by commission, sometimes of his own volition, he directed special efforts to arousing the American citizenry to its grave responsibilities at home and abroad. Although he himself was unscathed by the "Big Bust" of 1929, he saw what mass unemployment and mass misery could do to youth adrift; and he delivered in the fiction of that decade some of his most savage indictments of governmental apathy and public indifference to the plight of the younger generation.

Ironically, Tarkington's serious studies of adolescents are well-nigh forgotten, while his lighter pieces are still widely read. Under the sobering influence of the Depression, he made significant use of the themes which reflect a marked change in his attitude toward late adolescence as a subject for fiction. *Pretty Twenty*, for example, is a tender short novel which dramatizes a faith which Tarkington never lost in his native land. *Rennie Peddigoe*, another well-wrought novelette, lifts an idealistic young woman out of a ruthless Fitzgerald society to an emotional serenity and spiritual maturity denied her profligate parents. Perhaps the most penetrating study of this period is the initiation novel *This Boy Joe* (1933), which pits a boy just the age of Willie Baxter against a hostile world. In a climactic series of severe tests, young Joe is forced to reject his closest friend, to submit to a humiliating love affair, and to forego a lucrative job rather than abandon his integrity. Tarkington put into *This Boy Joe* the accumulated wisdom of a lifetime, only to have the text slashed for serialization. As a result, the reflective passages which gave substance to the story were omitted, and little more than a deliberately underwritten plot remains.

Today it is open to question whether the exhumation of Tarkington's studies of American adolescents in Depression days would add appreciably to his stature. *This Boy Joe*, for example, has yet to be republished in book form with the excised commentary. A new generation, alien to the motives which prompted the work, would probably be less perceptive of its merits today than were its editors then. "New ages breed new sages," the proverb goes, and particularly is this true of the fictionist who founds his stories upon the socio-economic situation of the hour. The social structure of the present-day Age of Affluence seems so remote from the poverty of four decades ago that Tarkington's insistence upon Emersonian idealism and old-time "rugged individualism" might be considered as hopelessly passé.

## II  *Writing for a Double Audience*

Both early and late, it is evident that the wily novelist was directing his tales at a double audience—adults as well as children. The language in *Penrod*, for instance, is frequently beyond many a twelve-year-old boy. The mongrel Duke, Penrod's "wistful dog," is described as "obviously the result of a series of mesalliances." When Penrod is spanked by his father, the text reads: "Mr. Schofield came, and shortly thereafter, there was put into practice an old patriarchal custom. It is a custom of inconceivable antiquity: probably primordial, certainly prehistoric, but still in vogue in some remaining citadels of the ancient simplicities of the Republic."[12] And when Penrod buys gumdrops, this delicacy is described as "consisting for the most part of the heavily flavoured hoofs of horned cattle, but undeniably substantial and so generously capable of resisting solution that the purchaser must need be avaricious beyond reason who did not realize his money's worth."[13] Even foreign words like "belles lettres," "duello," and "ennui" are found on the same page in this work. These samples, selected at random, could be continued *ad libitum*. Hardly typical of "children's literature," in the customary sense of the term, such circumlocutions and foreign terms strongly suggest that Tarkington had adult readers as well as children in mind.

In other words, we might say that, in a work like *Penrod*, Tarkington sought to entertain the youngsters with the rout of his characters in a riot of situations, while still delighting older folks with his subtleties of style and theme. As Tarkington himself explained his objective, he tried to manage his story material in such a way that the juvenile reader could enjoy vicariously the escapades of Penrod and his cronies, while the adult reader could respond to Penrod's "suffering and his mental processes, not what happens to him." The dual goals of such an approach are an invitation for the unwary novelist to waver. In some instances, particularly in his later attempts, Tarkington comes close to disaster when he lets his gaze wander from this double objective. *Little Orvie* (1934) is perhaps the most conspicuous example; Orvie, a seven-year-old, is simply too young to reach either reader level, and the book fails.

Even the ingenious device of writing up to adults proved no safeguard for Tarkington's authorial reputation when he had attained recognition as a juvenile writer. Although the late William Lyon Phelps ranked Tarkington with Mark Twain and Stephen Crane as America's three greatest juvenile authors, the distinction has been a dubious one. Speaking of American letters in general, Van Wyck Brooks remarked in *The Writer in America* (1953), "It has often been said that our American literature is a literature for boys, or one might better say that Cooper, Irving, Longfellow, Dana . . . have largely survived as classics for adolescents."[14] Mentioning no names, Brooks then says that "Many writers of more recent years have suggested overgrown exuberant boys"—the motif for many a lament raised by the critics against Tarkington. Just prior to reading *Alice Adams*, Carl Van Doren had said that "In contemporary American fiction Mr. Tarkington is the perennial sophomore."[15] At the same time, James Branch Cabell asserted in *Beyond Life* (1921) that "The fact remains that out of forty-nine years of living Mr. Tarkington has thus far given us only *Seventeen*."[16]

As many an aspiring novelist has discovered, it is a redoubtable task to establish a "public image"; once fixed, however, it is next to impossible to change. Thus, after *Tom Sawyer,* Mark Twain was "the author of kids' stories"; after *Penrod,* Tarkington was tarred with Mark Twain's old brush. As Grant Overton admitted in "Totalling Mr. Tarkington" (1924), "this adolescent in literature [Penrod] gave his fashioner a distinct setback."[17] By implication, that is, any book for or about juveniles is automatically considered slight by the critics. Edith Wyatt, in her review of *Gentle Julia* (1922), first deplored the scarcity of competent American writers in this field; then she confessed that "Even those who possess any technique here have commanded little appreciation for it."[18] Yet, when we glance down the list of perennial favorites in this category, we are struck by two things: one, the brevity of the list; and, two, the quality of the writers on it. It would appear that the capacity to tell a lasting tale of this type is restricted to a favored few adults possessing a dualistic insight by which they can peer into youthful minds. Or, to permit Tarkington's pioneer biographer, Robert Holliday, to change the figure: "It is as if the author had a device in his head like the plumbing giving hot and cold water to a bath-tub, and as if he could at will turn off the stream of mature thinking and turn on the boy thinking." As Holliday intimates, this is no mean ability: "To recapture the sensations of twelve or of seventeen is exactly what the average adult mind cannot do. . . . For the production of Tarkington's boy stories something else was required beyond stylistic skill, something like genius."[19]

### III   *The Proprieties of Realism*

From another angle, detractors of Tarkington's juvenile writings have occasionally accused him of undue reticence in depicting the crude or vulgar about "real-life" youngsters. Among such characters, there is a complete absence of curiosity about sex, for example; there is a similar absence of profanity. No reader could possibly be embarrassed by the predicaments of Tarkington's offspring from early childhood through late adolescence. Again, we need not look far for explanations: Tarkington was the selective realist who rejected many subject areas as inappropriate for novelistic treatment (especially for young readers); he also rejected gross language and a gutter style for similar reasons. We might also add that his own youthful experiences and subsequent observations did not dwell long in such regions; hence, he filled no reservoir to draw from even had he wished. Unlike Stephen Crane, Tarkington did not go to the Bowery to find his young rapscallions; for his taste, he found plenty in his own neighborhood.

Yet, as sincere respecters of truth in their writings, both Crane and Tarkington were compelled by the same motivation in their delineation of youth—to write about "real boys doing real things." Of Crane, William Lyon Phelps writes in his Introduction to the *Whilomville Stories*, "Stephen Crane exercised the same art on boys and girls that he displayed in dealing with soldiers or with the vagabonds in city slums. There is the same remorseless and uncompromising love of truth."[20] For his part, as Woodress observes, "Tarkington too had firm ideas of what boy life really was like and relegated most stories of children to the limbo of claptrappery."[21]

This point raises the same issue in miniature over which Tarkington fought all his life with the Naturalist school of fiction. To Tarkington, Crane and his fellows upset the balance of reality one way; Tarkington himself has often been accused of tipping it too far in the other direction. In an article, "Booth Tarkington: Time for Revival" (1954), Richard Crowley expatiates on this score: "Critics in the past have refused to take these works (like *Penrod* and *Seventeen*) seriously, considering them 'superficial,' and accusing Tarkington of deliberately avoiding the 'real' problems of the teen-ager, such as growing sex awareness. This attitude seems to me to be simply critical snobbishness. Penrod and Willie Baxter are no more superficial than Tom Sawyer or Huck Finn, or, for that matter, David Copperfield." After all, Crowley concludes, "there is as much sunshine as gloom in the adolescent life, and there is no reason why a writer should have to examine this age group with the depressing detachment of an Albert Moravia in order to have his work taken seriously. The problems that beset Tarkington's youths are the same problems that harass normal young men everywhere. Their romantic escapades should continue to be read with a kindred understanding and sympathy as long as there are normal young men to read about them."[22]

## IV   *The Year of Decisions*

Tarkington's exploitation of youthful adventures began at a critical period in his career; indeed, the year 1912 proved to be a pivotal one in several respects. In the early months two oppressive clouds lifted; the divorce proceedings for his first marriage were completed, and he shook off an incipient alcoholism. Of equal importance to the novelist, he regained his old delight in writing. By early autumn he could write his editor at *Harper's*, "Now I'm in condition as I was ten years ago, but with a very piquant realization of wasted time. . . . I want to make up for that time & I have the energy to do it, & the 'stuff' stored. I don't want to lose any more time."[23]

The first product of the revitalized Tarkington was "Mary Smith," a whimsical short story of frustrated adolescence closely akin to a later *Seventeen*. This story was followed immediately by *The Flirt*, the first of Tarkington's "Indianapolis stories" and the advance work of his mature efforts. Though far from the forefront in the Tarkington canon, *The Flirt* is still worthy of note. As mentioned before, it introduced in Cora Madison the earliest of several *femmes fatales* who figure in subsequent novels. More importantly, despite its melodramatic moments, it marks Tarkington's tentative entry into realistic fiction based upon intimate observation of the local scene. Finally, it begot in Hedrick Madison, Cora's younger brother, the first of Tarkington's juveniles and the predecessor of Penrod Schofield. More the *enfant terrible* than Penrod ever becomes, Hedrick displays a naïve cruelty which is still quite in keeping with Tarkington's concept of young animals. On the other hand, like so many of Tarkington's budding rogues, Hedrick is a gallant gentleman at heart—and he clearly captured the heart of his creator as well.

Even while seeing *The Flirt* through preparations for installment publication, Tarkington was rebounding from the depths of divorce into the upper realms of romance. While attending a dinner party five years earlier, he had been introduced to

Susanah Robinson of Dayton, Ohio. Though they had met again briefly but once, he called upon her soon after his divorce. Then began a whirlwind courtship of ten months (during which he promised to give up drinking), and on November 6, 1912, the Indianapolis *News* announced their marriage. This alliance was the beginning of a completely happy relationship for the next thirty-three years.

A generous chapter could not describe the manifold influences exerted by Susanah Tarkington upon the life and letters of her husband. In the first place, she entered his life at a time when he was most in need of her calm, her talents, her direction. Schooled by practical necessity before her marriage, she had made a success in the business world. Esconced in her new home, she proved herself an able hostess, a delightful conversationalist, a gracious lady. Most important to Tarkington at this time, she was a wife who was unstintingly devoted to her husband and acutely perceptive about his needs. With disarming diplomacy, she relieved him of the household burdens and nagging distractions which had grown apace during his problem period. Even when Tarkington's *ménage* increased with income and fame to houses in Maine and Indiana, plus a retinue of half a dozen servants, she directed the household with tactful efficiency. As Woodress sums it up, "Susanah Tarkington became companion and manager for her novelist-husband; and if the first decade after their marriage resulted in a richly creative period, she was more than a little responsible."[24]

## V  *The Origin of Penrod*

In circumstances strongly reminiscent of the James Fenimore Cooper legend, Susanah Tarkington promoted her husband's interest in juvenile writing which had emerged briefly in "Mary Smith" and *The Flirt*. Not long after they had settled in the old home at 1100 North Pennsylvania Street, Mrs. Tarkington whiled away a winter afternoon reading *The Hill* by Horace Vachell. This British novel about student life at Harrow describes poignantly the hazing and flogging so common in an earlier day, and it moved her strongly. When she took the novel to her husband to read, he granted the authenticity of the bullying by the older boys but asserted that "no boy ever talked like the puppets in that story." To this pronouncement, Susanah Tarkington issued to her husband almost verbatim the same challenge which Susan DeLancey Cooper had tendered her husband a century before: "Why don't you write about boys as they really are?"

Some two or three weeks later, Tarkington called his wife into his workroom and read to her "Penrod and the Pageant." Although at the time neither suspected it, this manuscript was to become far more than Tarkington's response to his wife's invitation. Not only was it the first of the lucrative Penrod adventures; it was also a long step toward Tarkington's becoming a familiar American figure. During the sixty years since Penrod's birth, he has established himself among that select company of folk heroes who comprise the core of our native literary tradition. Among the ranks of our most familiar figures, he strides beside Rip Van Winkle, Leatherstocking, Huck Finn, and Holden Caulfield.

It is almost a cliché to say that "There is something of Penrod in every man and much of Tarkington in Penrod." To trace Tarkington's adaptations of boyhood memories through the pages of *Penrod* and elsewhere would lead far afield into matters of much amusement but of little moment. For present purposes, it must suffice to say that Tarkington coupled an acutely retentive memory to a highly creative imagination. The latter was frequently assisted by the direct observation of his three young Jameson nephews and their neighborhood gang. All of these resources, it must be said, are limited to the middle-class society of the Midwest. Tarkington himself insisted that any man could relive his own boyhood in *Penrod* "unless he lived in the east side of New York or went yachting out of Newport." It is doubtful that such a claim was ever literally true; certainly, one could not make it today. As noted before, the United States at the three-quarter century mark is far removed at all age levels from the pre-World War I days of Penrod and Sam.

On the other hand, the Penrod stories have enjoyed a popularity which has kept them in print from their serial publication in *Everybody's Magazine* in 1913 to this day. When the tales were brought out in book form in 1914 by Doubleday, Page and Company, the volume soon was established as a best-seller in the *Bookman* lists; in *Golden Multitudes,* Frank Luther Mott lists *Penrod* as one of three best-sellers for 1914 (each with a required sale of 900,000 copies). Royalties from the combined publications of the Penrod stories in both magazine serial and book form rapidly swelled the Tarkington exchequer to startling proportions. Tarkington himself was almost embarrassed by his new fortune. In a letter to his long-time friend and collaborator, Julian Street, he confessed, "My prices astonish me; they've climbed steadily, by offers, until I'm rather sorry for the magazines that pay 'em. I've never really asked any particular price: the thing has somehow just done itself."[25] (During the Depression, he voluntarily cut his rate for the *Saturday Evening Post.*) One of his chief delights from this new affluence was the opportunity it afforded him to return to his beloved Kennebunkport, Maine, and establish summer quarters in "the house that Penrod built."

Other reasons that account for the phenomenal success of the Penrod stories are not difficult to find. Stylistically speaking, Tarkington by this time was a master of his craft. Descriptive details rise naturally from each situation, the narrative flow is free and smooth, the characters spring quickly into focus. In his determination to maintain excellence even in his juvenile writings, Tarkington took great pains to infuse freshness into the comic situations. "One main thing is to keep out . . . hand-me-down boy humor," he warned his colleagues while the dramatization of *Penrod* was underway. In addition, as noted, the dialogue among the boys is on a near-adult level; in this respect, however, Tarkington had his own convictions. "'Boy writers' depend on "Gee, Fellers' and 'Say, kids' and 'Kid nicknames,'" he explained; "if you'll notice I have utterly avoided this stock stuff . . . even though most kids actually do say 'Say, kids' and 'Gee.'"[26] In other efforts to avoid "stock stuff," Tarkington labored to exploit the commonplace, the typical, and even the prosaic rather than to resort to cheap melodrama for reader interest. Consequently, the Penrod stories evoke American boyhood realistically because the boys are real people. As Tarkington himself assessed the work, "*Penrod* has been a success, because it has kept to *true* boy and avoided book-and-stage boy."[27]

## VI   *The Structuring of Juvenilia*

In the conventional sense of the term, it is perhaps a misnomer to label *Penrod, Penrod and Sam, Penrod Jashber, Seventeen, Little Orvie,* even *Gentle Julia* as "novels." The element of plot, for example, is always minimal in Tarkington's juvenile works in order that major emphasis may be placed upon individual characters in limited situations. For this reason, he titled the stories in this category after dominant figures instead of for principal events. Even while acknowledging his indebtedness to Mark Twain for a masterpiece like *Tom Sawyer,* Tarkington observed, "Tom and Huck are realistic only in character. He [Twain] gave 'em what boys don't get, when it came to 'plot.'" Sensing that much in the Twain story was belated wish-fulfillment, Tarkington concluded, "All that the boy Sam had wished to happen, he [Twain] made happen."[28] When Tarkington began to draw from his own boyhood memories for story material, he realized that the keenest recall is a selective process which evokes only the discontinuity of self-contained incidents.

Soon after *Seventeen* had entrenched itself as a modern American classic of its genre, critic Blanche Colton Williams declared flatly that Tarkington's teen tales lacked plot. And, in the usual sense of the word, she is quite right. What she failed to realize is that the author designed them that way. As a perceptive craftsman, it was obvious to him that any narrative deliberately overwritten for the thrills of a sensational plot, yet underwritten in literary style or thematic substance, was doomed to a brief life. Surveying the titles popular among children sixty years ago, he noted especially the early death of topical adventure based on current events, glamorous inventions, or contemporary figures. Founded on such ephemera, even the better books for children had their flash of glory and then died in obscurity. Also, as he well knew, few adults would find a juvenile story-line sufficiently interesting to merit their attention. Consequently, Tarkington deliberately sacrificed "plot" for other considerations which he deemed more important.

Instead, Tarkington's juvenile writings can be best described as "linear narration." In accordance with this technique, normal chronology controls the sequence of events, each incident evolves in logical order, and the conclusion of any movement is merely the termination of the action. In general, each incident is complete within itself, although some centralizing theme (like the puppy-love of Willie Baxter in *Seventeen*) may give a surface unity to the story. Tarkington found this construction not only eminently suitable for young readers and the demands of serial publication but also illustrative of a basic Tarkington theory concerning the nature of juvenile literature. To his mind, youngsters lack not only the capacity but the volition to take "the long view" implicit in the full-blown novel. For them, life is a succession of presents, each complete in itself. As Tarkington phrased it, "to the eye of youth, time is not really fleeting, time is long—so long that for practical uses the present appears to be permanent."[29] In his stories, therefore, his children pass from one escapade to another; yesterday is forgotten in the urgency of today, and tomorrow is but an uneasy cloud on a distant horizon.

As a rule, Tarkington noted, a child's world is elemental, simple—the adult world about him makes it so. A fictional account of a child's life becomes, therefore, unreal the moment an extraneous complexity is contrived by an author. As observed before, Tarkington sought to do no more than evoke a credible American childhood by creating ordinary characters who do ordinary things—in extraordinary ways. He was quite aware that whatever appeal his stories might have lay elsewhere than in sheer narrative. When a runaway *Penrod* was under consideration for dramatization, its author was skeptical of its stage possibilities. "The detail—*not plot*—is what has made it [a bestseller]," he wrote George Tyler, his New York producer who was urging the play adaptation. Over the protests of the novelist, *Penrod* and other Tarkington juvenile pieces did "hit the boards" (and subsequently were made into motion pictures); but their originator would be the first to admit that the relationship between these dramatized versions and their forebears is rarely closer than that of a first cousin. In each instance, a trumped-up situation had to be devised into which Tarkington's characters and incidents were fitted more as accessories than principals.

Fortunately for Tarkington's juvenile fiction, the limitations of serial publication worked little hardship on these youthful studies. Compartmentalized within separate units, each episode constitutes an entity within itself. To add to the illusion of unity, each installment consists of four to six separate, labeled chapters. A brief analysis of the opening anecdote in *Penrod* illustrates the pattern which Tarkington followed: Chapter I presents the plight of Penrod the forenoon prior to "The Pageant of the Table Round," Chapter II describes his elaborate escapist device, Chapter III outfits the victim for the ordeal, Chapter IV starkly reveals the crisis confronting Penrod, Chapter V dramatizes his desperate solution, and Chapter VI leaves him chastised and chastened that evening. In a reminiscent moment he sighs mournfully to his dog, Duke, "Well, hasn't this been a day!" Soon, as twilight draws on and a star appears, Penrod responds with a yawn. "Then he sighed once more, but not reminiscently: evening had come, the day was over. It was a sigh of pure ennui." Chapter VII begins, "Next day . . . ," and Penrod is off to battle "The Evils of Drink."

## VII    *The Uses of Reverie*

A frequent component in the Tarkington formula for juvenile fiction is a James Thurber escape mechanism known as reverie. Tarkington's "gift in the expression of daydreams," as Edith Wyatt termed it, gained for him some of his finest comic effects. In a review of *Gentle Julia* (1922), Elmer Adams became one of the first to identify for critical recognition this device in Tarkington's writings. At that time Adams wrote, "One of Tarkington's special gifts is in the use of reverie. . . . These monstrous, unbridled imaginings of youth Tarkington has shown in all their grotesqueness, and in their relation to what may be called the higher reasoning faculties of the individual and his character and actions."[30]

Removed from context, words in the above quotation like "monstrous," "unbridled," and "grotesqueness" may mislead the unwary. Rather than using reverie as a psychoanalytical lever with which to pry into dark recesses of depravity, Tarkington employed the device as one way of allowing his repressed children to indulge in typical William Steig "dreams of glory." As Adams also said, "Whereas others use the method of psychoanalysis to reveal people's innate baseness, Tarkington uses it to bring out the unsophistication and innocence of certain types."[31] Invariably, these "certain types" are underdog characters from twelve to twenty-two who suffer from the constant humiliation of adult superiority. The younger they are, the more "monstrous and unbridled" their daydreams become; but at no point does the "grotesque" with Tarkington assume the implications of the term as used in regard to Sherwood Anderson's characters in *Winesburg, Ohio*.

Tarkington himself describes the nature of these reveries in an early chapter of *Penrod*. "Maturity forgets the marvellous realness of a boy's day-dreams," he observed, "how colourful they glow, rosy and living, and how opaque the curtain closing down between the dreamer and the actual world." When Penrod is overcome by "the nervous monotony of the schoolroom," he indulges in a flight of fancy. In his case, of course, since "every boy's fundamental desire is to do something astonishing himself, so as to be the centre of all human interest and awe, it was natural that Penrod should discover in fancy the delightful secret of self-levitation."[32] With all the ease of Sam Small, the "Flying Yorkshireman" created by Eric Knight, Penrod soars high above the confines of the classroom, high above the gaping city throng, but well in view of Marjorie Jones "of the amber curls and the golden voice." Returned to earth by a stolid schoolmarm, Penrod resorts to another type of romanticizing, lying, in his efforts to survive in an adult world. Sad to relate, his most ingenious fabrication leads only to a trip to the woodshed with another imperceptive grown-up.

The most frequent motivation behind the daydreams in Tarkington's juvenile stories is love. Flouted by the disdainful Marjorie as "the Worst Boy in Town," Penrod stumbles along the path to romance in lonely rejection. Buoyed by the fancy of self-levitation, however, "he floated in through the window of her classroom and swam gently along the ceiling like an escaped toy balloon." Sweet dream of youth! Now Marjorie "fell upon her knees beside her little desk, and, lifting up her arms toward him, cried with love and admiration, 'Oh, *Penrod!*'" And now Penrod "negligently kicked a globe from the high chandelier, and, smiling coldly, floated out through the hall to the front steps of the school, while Marjorie followed, imploring him to grant her one kind look."[33]

Five years later in *Seventeen*, we find Willie Baxter in the same situation. So dazed is Willie by infatuation for his "Baby-talk Lady" that only occasionally does reality swim into his view. After his first traumatic encounter with the unknown Lola Pratt and Flopit, her fluffy canine companion, Willie "suffered from breathlessness and from pressure on the diaphragm" during the remainder of an agonizing summer. At one point, he "fell into a kind of stupor; vague, beautiful pictures rising before him, and one least blurred being of himself, on horseback, sweeping between Flopit and a racing automobile. And then, having restored the little animal to its mistress, William sat carelessly in the saddle (he had the Guardsman's seat) while the perfectly trained steed wheeled about, forelegs in the air, preparing to go. 'But shall I not see you again, to thank you more properly?' she cried, pleading. 'Some other day—perhaps,' he answered. And left her in a cloud of dust."[34] Like Penrod, Willie has his dreams of glory on the battlefield of love. In *Seventeen*, however, the campaign for Milady's heart dominates everything about the novel. The various stratagems contrived by Willie to ensnare Miss Pratt result in the same episodic structure described in relation to *Penrod*, and most of the other stylistic characteristics of the earlier works also are preserved.

Even the next stage in "the seven ages of man" is not without its daydreams. In *Gentle Julia*, a trio of belligerent young males contest for the favors of Miss Julia Atwater (whose only flaw is "a heart kinder than most"). Among these young men is Noble Dill, whose case of lovesickness shares most of the sorest symptoms of fifteenth-century Courtly Love. Not only must the hero pit his meager force against the ardent might of his competitors and the vagrant heart of Julia, but he must deal with a father who identifies the personality of the young suitor with his Orduma Egyptian Cigarettes—aromatic but mild. Not without reason, Mr. Atwater is scornful of Noble's *esprit de coeur*, as well as of his probable salary in the insurance business. Noble himself "had doubts about being able to show Mr. Atwater anything important connected with the cigarette or the salary, but he *could* prove how reckless he was." The immediate problem, of course, is how. As he ponders the issue, "a vision formed before him: he saw Julia and her father standing spellbound at a crossing while a smiling youth stood directly between the rails in the middle of the street and let a charging trolley-car destroy him—not instantly, for he would live long enough to whisper, as the stricken pair bent over him: 'Now, Julia, which do you believe: your father or me?' And then with a slight, dying sneer: 'Well, Mr. Atwater, is this reckless enough to *suit* you?' "[35] Thus Noble Dill joins that inglorious company of Tarkington males who seek to soften the blows of love by the solace of reverie. Although each learns that such dreams come to naught, they serve a worthy end for the novelist.

## VIII    *The Uses of Humor*

For Tarkington, this end is the achievement of some of his choicest humorous effects. Whatever his hapless males conjure up is always so remote from possibility that only the ridiculous results. The eye of the reader cannot but twinkle as Penrod swoops above the cheering crowd or as Willie Baxter plunges past on his noble steed. Thus revealed in the stark light of comedy, these Tarkington figures emerge as romantics *par excellence*; the strongest colors of their daydreams are bright with humor. Though tinged with pathos, none shows its subject demeaned by low passions or base drives. Tarkington noted in *Penrod* that "the normal boy is always at least one half Barnum." The show-off in a Tarkington tale is a quite typical youngster seeking the approbation of his peers, resenting the duress of parental authority, releasing the animal spirits impounded by school or society. When he loses his balance, the pratfall is pure slapstick; when he does not, his triumph, too, is pure joy.

Much of the humor in Tarkington's juvenile stories might aptly be labeled "situation comedy." In general, his narrative pattern places the hero amid a dilemma with no foreseeable outlet or within a vise of circumstances with no conceivable escape. Thus Penrod is thrust before the public gaze at the pageant while garbed in unmentionables, he is doomed to escort

Baby Rennsdale to the cotillion, or he is ensnared by his own ingenuity when Georgie Bassett undergoes "'nishiation for the In-Or-In." Driven by fate into crisis after crisis, Penrod must resort to amazing stratagems—and thereby he induces amused reactions from the reader. It is apparent that this type of limited action within a limited situation was ideally suited for the serialized form of the original stories. Though a crafty Mr. Tarkington sometimes led Penrod to the woodshed and sometimes to the corner ice-cream parlor by way of anticlimax, he did not do so until earlier there had been an unmistakable climax.

Tarkington's deft descriptive touch was never so sure as when he sketched minor comic figures. Whenever practicable while dealing with these peripheral characters, Tarkington utilized traits identified by direct sensory appeal. In one instance it may be the indescribable "semi-syllables" of Verman, the little Negro boy with the harelip in *Penrod*; another time it may be the undulating bulk of Kitty, the Atwater's cook in *Gentle Julia*. It may even be the "passion for bread-and-butter, covered with apple sauce and powdered sugar" which besets Janie Baxter so often in *Seventeen*; or perhaps it may be the insistent aroma of Orduma Egyptian Cigarettes which trails Noble Dill through the pages of *Gentle Julia*. Whatever the tag, it is fastened early upon its bearer, and it is worn from then on. Although Tarkington rarely overused a good thing once he had it, he realized the role of recognition in comedy. On the juvenile level, an especially high level of consistency is vital to the impact potential of these minor characters who contribute substantially to the humorous aspects of the story.

Also on the lighter side of his juvenile fiction, Tarkington employed the art of gentle shock, one inflicted on the reader by the wrongdoing of the youngsters. For the most part, this shock results from the reader's wicked sense of approval upon observing a naughty deed he himself would like to have done. Thus, when Penrod's father confiscates the boy's concertina, Penrod promptly throws his arithmetic book down the cistern, and the result is humorous—just as it is when Penrod "fumbles in the wrong pocket" for his Sunday-School dime, then spends it later on gumdrops and a forbidden Sabbath movie. Such incidents could be multiplied at length, for Tarkington used every variation of this device. Like Huck Finn before them, his young rebels from twelve to twenty-two indulge in furtive smoking and in petty larceny; indeed, prevarication, deceit, expedient dishonesty are more the rule than the exception in their lives. The good things in life like school (public school, Sunday School, dancing school, *any* school), parental concern, polite manners—indeed, the social order in general—suffer badly at the hands of Tarkington upstarts. Yet, we must not be misled by the evidence; whatever the transgression may be, everything is done without malice. Tarkington's juveniles are not delinquents; their revolt against an oppressive adult society is never dangerous. In those bygone days, the worse the misbehavior of the youngsters, the more hilarious the fun.

Whereas most of Tarkington's juvenile writings deal with frustrated masculinity, no little of their hilarity may be credited to the feminine element. Immediately, however, we note an odd anomaly in the Tarkington touch—although in his social novels he drew a broad spread of female characters with devastating precision, the girls in his juvenilia are surprisingly oversimplified. Indeed, categorically speaking, they tend to divide rather easily into one group of ultrafeminists and another group of tomboys. That is, they are either the pink-and-white perfection of Marjorie Jones in *Penrod* or the jelly-smeared griminess of Florence Atwater in *Gentle Julia*.

We can only speculate upon this strange discrepancy, for the clues are meager. A possible lead is the family situation of Tarkington himself: Hauté was more mother than sister, his daughter, Laurel, was reared by her mother from infancy, and he gained only nephews from Hauté's marriage. His unfinished autobiography, *As I Seem to Me* (1941), provides ample evidence that his childhood playmates were nearly all boys; and a lengthy article on "What I Have Learned from Boys" (1925) was never matched by one on "What I Have Learned from Girls." In short, he may have felt some inadequacy in dealing with female youngsters from sheer lack of direct observation.

Among the first category, "amber-curled and beautiful Marjorie Jones," the *inamorata* of Penrod, almost rises to reality upon rare occasions; for the most part, however, she dwells on a rarefied plane well beyond Penrod's grubby reach. Although she figures prominently in several of the more harrowing episodes, she remains but a contributive character. Visibly perfect in her well-starched femininity, Marjorie serves mainly to highlight the rueful boyness of a beleaguered Penrod. Her senior by five years, the irresistible Lola Pratt in *Seventeen*, is cut from the same bolt. Like Marjorie, Miss Pratt delights in flounces and frills, carries with her "a rosy glamor" fatal to nearby males, and accepts the homage due her with piquant condescension. The infatuation of William Sylvanus Baxter with this vision of loveliness is painfully evident; Lola's love for Lola is equally obvious. Wise beyond the years of those who fall beneath her spell, she "knew how to do her work but too well." Tarkington remarks that Lola, at her first encounter with Willie, "might have reminded a much older boy than Willie of a spotless white kitten"; but, before her departure, Tarkington injects something of the vixen into this calculating flirt who seems so soft and kittenish. Before the summer fades, the reader knows her every artifice, her every trick; indeed, he has to marvel at the sweeping success of her campaign. For Miss Pratt came, she was seen, and she conquered; such is her role in *Seventeen*.

Willie's kid sister, on the other hand, is in the other category of young females in Tarkington's fictional families. Janie Baxter, the irrepressible brat of *Seventeen*, is pure tomboy. To her brother's acute embarrassment, she is completely uninhibited, dismayingly direct. And, to the reader's delight, she is wholly without principle. Janie spies upon Willie without a pang, unashamedly concocts livid tales about him, and gives the poor boy neither privacy nor peace. Yet Janie is not a mean child by nature, nor is she vicious in her actions. Even as William feels borne down by the weight of his superiors, so does Janie resent her brother's struggle to keep her in her place. Not infrequently, as a matter of fact, she brings William back from the world of fantasy, although as an escort she eschews finesse. Like her male counterparts, Janie loves most her moments of glory when she dramatizes to her mother what she overheard while spying in the bushes or squatting beneath a window. She is glad to repeat Mr. Parcher's eloquent profanity, imitate Miss Pratt's baby talk, or rehearse Willie's discourse on love. True, she has no scruples, no respect for the proprieties, not the veriest shred of good judgment. Yet, even after committing the unpardonable sin of shaming brother William before Lola as he bids her a last good-bye, Janie confesses to him, " 'Willie, I told mamma I was sorry I made you feel so bad.' " And when her brother, bereft of light and love, "uttered a sigh, so hoarse, so deep from the tombs, so prolonged, that Jane . . . sat up straight with a jerk," Tarkington reports kindly, "she was wise enough not to speak."[36] To the end, she is simply Willie's kid sister; and she labors diligently to fulfill every aspect of a demanding role.

The direct linear descendant of Janie Baxter is Florence Atwater. Ostensibly, the heroine of *Gentle Julia* is the beauteous young aunt of Florence from whom the novel derives its name. At an eligible twenty years of age, Miss Julia Atwater is besieged by a company of determined suitors, and the least among them is Mr. Noble Dill. As Woodress summarizes the situation, at a dauntless thirteen years of age "Florence unaccountably undertakes to promote his interests—and thereby hangs the tale."[37] *Gentle Julia* is unadulterated summer fare, and Florence is a thoroughly lovable young hoyden. She flits through the pages of the novel like Ariel of old—impish, mischievous, "tricksy"; yet, at the close, we must say with Prospero, "Thou hast done well, fine Florence!" Against odds of two to one, she teases her male contemporaries without mercy, outwits them without shame, yet creates nothing but hilarity from the havoc she works. We suspect that Florence so captured the paternal love of Tarkington that he allowed her to get away with most of the story. Be that as it may, she certainly is the minor dynamo who sparks the major interest in this delightful novel. Were it not for her, we could hardly mention *Gentle Julia* among Tarkington's juvenile writings; with her, however, it hardly can be excluded.

After the publication of *The Flirt* in 1912, scarcely a novel emerged from Tarkington's pen without some sketch of childhood within its pages. Young George Minafer in *The Magnificent Ambersons* is shown in several masterly scenes; even *The Midlander* has a memorable opening chapter contrasting the personalities of Dan and Harlan Oliphant as children. Other novels, such as *Mary's Neck* and *Ramsey Milholland,* likewise contain scattered juvenilia; indeed, the younger generation encroaches upon a sizable proportion of his total output.

It is a credit to Tarkington the artist that the infusion of this youthful element into his mature works does not detract from their distinction. In fact, more often than not, the childhood escapades in these novels provide an accurate index of those very traits which later shape the destinies of the characters who dominate these studies. Particularly in those works complicated by a long passage of time, such centralizing attributes offer a ready device whereby to preserve the unity of the novels. In some instances, like that of George's arrogance in *The Magnificent Ambersons,* a dominant characteristic may even generate the major emotional impact upon the reader.

Until late in life, Tarkington returned often to juvenile fiction. As he admitted on many occasions, he enjoyed writing about the younger generation; and, as he demonstrated with many a title, he also enjoyed a special genius for dealing with this subject area. Surely it is to the credit of Tarkington the man that he did not permit his talents to become prostituted by a debased style or stultified by easy formulas. Measured by whatever criteria, Tarkington remains a major figure in the writing of juvenilia.

CHAPTER 7

# The Final Accounting

IN many respects, the last quarter-century of Tarkington's
career constitutes the most pleasant years of a long lifetime
on the American literary scene. As the recipient of two Pulitzer
Prizes and a host of other distinctions, a place of prominence
in his national letters seemed reserved for him. The academic
world had offered him more honorary degrees than he felt he
should accept, and the publishing world was equally generous
in its plaudits. From his colleagues, he received in 1933 the
gold medal of the National Institute of Arts and Letters, which
had been awarded previously to Howells and Edith Wharton;
and in 1945 he was given the William Dean Howells medal,
awarded only once in five years by the American Academy of
Arts and Letters. One critical clique seemed eager to assign
him a place within the venerable hall of the "genteel realists"
alongside William Dean Howells, Henry James, and Edith
Wharton. The other school of critics was anxious to align him
with "novelists of social concern" in company with early figures
like Robert Herrick and Theodore Dreiser and with contemporary writers like Sinclair Lewis and Sherwood Anderson.

Furthermore, the vexing problem of making a livelihood was
solved. His name on a manuscript was an entrée to almost any
editorial office, and he could command his own rates. Royalties
from his best-sellers earned him a handsome income, although
they made up but a fraction of the whole. Film rights, radio
rights, reprint rights, plus the return from a steady stream of
fresh efforts, built Tarkington a fortune from writing which
was probably unequaled by any other author of that time in
the United States. Even the Depression proved a boon for him;

125

his stories remained in constant demand, his rate stayed so high he cut it himself, and his dollars bought much more than normal in a deflated economy.

In addition, Tarkington was blessed by congenial surroundings. His marriage to Susanah continued to be a constant source of wonder to him in its wealth of cordial compatibility. Through one connection or another, he continually expanded his circle of friendships, for he possessed a happy talent for making new friendships while keeping the old. Some of these resulted from travels which ranged from South Africa to the British Isles; others came from the stage or his ever-widening world of art. Also, he rejoiced in the new additions to the family clan which his sister and her children contributed from time to time.

## I  *The Conquest of Affliction*

All in all, the surface of the picture seems serene enough— and in many ways it was; but beneath that surface ran cross-currents of distress. Although his mother had died suddenly of a heart attack in 1909, Tarkington's father had continued his kindly role in the household until the age of ninety. In a tightly knit family like the Tarkingtons, the death of the aged judge in January 1923 came as a sharp blow. To make the situation worse, Tarkington's sister, Hauté Jameson, was seriously ill at the time of their father's death. Mrs. Jameson, a born manager, surely would have been missed in making the funeral arrangements had it not been for Susanah's sustaining influence. The death of his father was hard for Tarkington to bear, for he and "Papa John" had shared a close relationship. As Tarkington wrote Hamlin Garland, his father always had been "the blessing of the lives of all his family."

Amid sorrow over his dying father and concern for his ill sister, still another tragedy struck Tarkington that fateful winter. Part of the previous summer at Kennebunkport he had shared with Laurel, his sixteen-year-old daughter by his previous marriage. Shortly after Laurel returned to boarding school that fall, she learned that she would soon no longer be an only child. Tarkington's first wife, Louisa, had also remarried and was expecting a baby. During the Christmas holidays, Laurel felt that her mother's affection for her had been supplanted by the new arrival, said so in extravagant terms, and was packed off to the Tarkingtons. Fancying that she had been banished by her mother, Laurel sank into deep depression as the winter advanced. Spring brought a severe case of pneumonia, to which she succumbed on April 18, 1923. The next day Tarkington wrote his long-time friend George Tyler, "yesterday afternoon, about five o'clock, Laurel had them call me in—and said 'Goodnight.'" In the same note he explained, "You see the *instrument* of the spirit had become maimed; the spirit could not endure to remain in the instrument after that."[1]

It is difficult for the outsider to realize that during that harrowing winter and spring Tarkington was working on *The Midlander*. Despite the tragic family conditions which prevailed, despite a month-long program of major dentistry, he adhered to his own gospel on the therapy of work. Actually, the novel proved to be his salvation. Already past the April deadline, he wrote in mid-May, "I must work: I must go on with this novel. If I shouldn't, I'd be wrecked, I think." Work he did; in a progress report of only four weeks later, he declared: "This work has just about saved me from ship-wreck. It's been hard to do it, but it would have been so much harder not to."[2] Autobiographical touches abound in *The Midlander*, but none is so poignant as the death scene of Dan Oliphant. At the moment that he died, "there was a look of startled incredulity— the look of one who suddenly recognizes . . . an old acquaintance long since disappeared but now abruptly returned."[3] Only a few short months before he delivered the manuscript in mid-July, Tarkington had written apropos of Laurel's death, "I think she went *somewhere* and that a day will come when I shall find her and she'll know all I've wanted so long to be to her."[4] Freethinker though he was throughout life, Tarkington never wavered in his faith in some form of immortality.

In this same cataclysmic period of 1922–23, Tarkington began a decade of desperate struggle to preserve his vision. Despite treatment for the cataracts, within another three years his left eye was useless, he had lost most of the sight in his right eye, and he was suffering severe headaches. When he finally was offered the choice between blindness and surgery, he capitulated to a series of futile operations. In spite of every effort, by the end of August 1930 Tarkington was totally blind. His right eye beyond cure, Tarkington took his last chance and had the cataract removed from his left eye. When the last bandages were slipped off in January 1931, Tarkington could see again; he had been almost blind for nearly three years and completely blind for over five months.

It is indicative of the man that there was no break in publication from 1929 to 1931. As a matter of fact, a whole new vista of subject matter opened for Tarkington—the Maine scene as he had come to love it in and around Kennebunkport. With typical artistic integrity, as one critic expresses these new efforts, "He handled this material with as much truth as he put into the Midwestern portraits of his earlier works."[5] Proverbial New England reticence is nowhere as marked as in the maritime regions of Maine, yet it is evident that Tarkington was genuinely respected and liked by the natives. Perhaps the reason lies in what the gardener in "High Summer" says of Joe Nutter, also a summer resident: "Just as cawman as the next man. Why I like Joe Nutter, it's because he's cawman."[6] In a wide variety of regional tales, ranging all the way from the high comedy of *Mary's Neck* to a moving study of manners in *Mirthful Haven*, a "cawman" Tarkington found Kennebunkport an uncommonly rewarding neighborhood. Despite the impairment of vision, his scenes of the seacoast appear in their true colors; and the acuity of his hearing seems keener than ever in the frequent lapses into local dialect.

## II   *The Drift toward Decadence*

As Tarkington viewed the sociocultural scene about him during the last two decades of his life, however, he needed no eye operation to detect much about which he had misgivings. E. S. Martin, in his comments about *The World Does Move* (1928), opens most of the issues with which this study of Tarkington will be concluded. Late in his review Martin observes, "The attraction of Mr. Tarkington's remarks in this book and of his books in general is that while he is full of humor and ministers to entertainment and is a story-teller and sees to it that his stories are readable, in the back of his mind he is a serious man, examining life with a deeper comprehension of its processes and proceedings than any other American writer now successfully implicated in the production of works of fiction. That is why one cares to listen to him speculating about the purpose and probable outcome of what is going on."[7] Some of the things that were "going on" in his day already have been considered, but a number await attention.

In almost every instance, a Tarkington cause is a lost cause. The debate of the critics over the merits of Howellsian Realism has long since been won by the libertarians of the contemporary school. The last strongholds for what might be termed "formalism" have largely yielded to the attrition of miscellaneous "isms" which stress "feeling" above "form." The final bastions of "the party of hope" (to borrow a phrase from Emerson) have largely fallen to the hedonism of the neo-pagans or to the futilitarianism of assorted cynics. Even "the American dream," as confirmed by Earl Tinker in *The Plutocrat*, has given way to "the Ugly American" in a world of errant values. For Tarkington, the surrender of such vital issues aroused serious qualms about the cultural drift of his day. Such an attitude, of course, labels Tarington a traditionalist—an infamous term to many a modern critic.

As remarked earlier, Tarkington numbered himself among the high majority of the "bourgeois gentility" to whom Naturalism in literature meant, as Maxwell Geismar explains, "novels of low-life, of crime, drink and vice, or the debased animal instincts in man."[8] Regardless of the original intention of its proponents to apply the study of environment and heredity to the province of the arts, Tarkington accepted the prevailing opinion which associated Naturalism with the extremes of radicalism. Given a clearer insight into the implications of the movement, he quite possibly would have supported much of its creed. As it was, on the basis of a partial judgment, he condemned the whole Naturalistic *Putsch* as an undisciplined rebellion. To his way of thinking, "The intelligent revolt against prettifying and too-sweet sweetness and sentimentality became in time indiscriminate, because continued rebellions always lose discrimination; and so it worked itself into a fury against whatever was pretty or sweet or had sentiment. Such a tumult, of course, couldn't sober down; but had to go to its own extremes, which, naturally, have proclaimed the worthiness of almost anything formerly thought ugly or sour or meaningless or in bad taste."[9]

In particular, Tarkington deplored a miscellany of "non-literary" subject areas which the new movement seemed to espouse. Among these were the profanity and obscenity which bulk so large in modern fiction. He saw no necessity in belaboring the Anglo-Saxon monosyllables in what he considered a childish attempt to seem grown-up. Ultimately, he hoped, a general attitude of disapproval would operate as a corrective upon literary license. After all, he pointed out, "Disgust is merely the other side of good taste, and without it we should never have had civilization or the arts, nor could we continue to enjoy them." Too many writers in recent times, he felt, have made a virtue of being disgusting; and their work has been praised by admirers as though it were extending the boundaries of literature. Such authors go on the assumption that nothing a man can do is unfit to be written about; consequently, Tarkington declared, "they guide their readers into every obscene nook and corner with a courageous indifference to everything that offends the senses, both physical and moral."[10] Needless to say, a course like this was anathema to "the gentleman from Indiana."

With biological determinism so prominent a factor in the Naturalist philosophy, sex emerged as a basic factor in fiction. Here again Tarkington had no quarrel about the importance of the subject itself. Always, he averred, the perceptive author must know every facet of life; on the other hand, his finer sensibilities should tell him that certain aspects of human behavior lie outside fictional treatment, that certain subject matter is simply nonliterary. In brief, the treatment of sex in literature is a matter of taste. Even at sixty years of age, the novelist declared, "There is not a thing you cannot talk about in a novel if you have good manners and know how to talk about it without dragging in the livery stable and the dissecting room. Still, some of these young writers, fond of discussing in a book what is not good manners to discuss in conversation, feel they must outwrite the anatomical textbooks."[11]

As might be expected, the restraint so evident elsewhere in

Tarkington comes into full play in this regard. He simply refused to "go all the way" in his love scenes. To use his own figure, "If a person stood in a pouring rain for an hour, there is no need to say that he got wet." In *The Flirt*, for example, when the passionate voice of Cora Madison whispers out of the dark, " 'Kiss me! Kiss me!' " Tarkington saw no demand for anatomical surveys or psychological analyses. When her paramour rejects Cora, he tells her plainly, " 'You love to fool yourself, Cora, but the role of betrayed virtue doesn't suit you very well. You're young, but you're a pretty experienced woman for all that, and you haven't done anything you didn't want to.' "[12] The mature reader may supply whatever details he wishes, for Tarkington preferred to concede to him a high degree of creative sensibility.

Examples of this "guilt by implication" technique are rife in Tarkington novels; basically, he was no prude. What he deplored was the erotic competition among authors who sought to grub ever deeper into the inviolable nature of man. Upon Tarkington's literary scale "the lowest form of writer," he who requires "the least craftsmanship," is the panderer to sensual thrills. "All he needs to know how to do is to describe scenes of sexual excitement with a few gross details, and he immediately clutches the kind of reader he is after."[13] In such a deromanticized literature, one in which sex equals love, Tarkington sensed the despiritualization of something inexpressibly beautiful into a biological act of evanescent thrills. Such an attitude, however, brought its problems. As early as 1927 he realized his own precarious position with respect to sexual liberties in fiction. The middle-ground position which he had held so long had become a no-man's-land open to attack from every quarter. As Tarkington wrote then, "In this new age of 'frankness in art' the old-fashioned liberal discovers that he is a puzzled conservative protesting against what appears to him a prevailing tainted ugliness, anything but frank. The moment he does protest, however, he encounters hot defenders of the new frankness: they assail him in the sacred name of Realism, and are loftily scornful of him."[14]

We should note not only Tarkington's identification of himself as a "liberal," but also his admission that criticism already has become "loftily scornful" of him. Although he had nearly twenty years of active authorship before him, Tarkington admitted then, "I suppose some of the ultra-moderns consider me a complacent old gentleman who has about shot his bolt."[15] Yet, despite mounting pressures, he never confused his distinction between love and sex; for, as far as he was concerned, sex did not even possess the virtue of novelty. "Spring is always Spring and youth is always youth," he observed, "although some of our more outspoken youth seem convinced that sex has been discovered in their own time and by them."[16] Although he conceded that some liberalization in attitudes toward sex might become socially beneficial, he felt that current tendencies toward exploiting the sordid could lead only to the denigration of a transcendently lovely theme.

Tarkington therefore drew no sketches of "fallen women" like Crane's *Maggie*; there are no "kept women" in the Dreiser tradition. As Carl Bennett observed, "There are indications that he could have produced work at least as shocking as *Sister Carrie, Jennie Gerhart,* or *The Financier,* and he most certainly would have done it with more literary art than Theodore Dreiser displayed."[17] The fact remains that Tarkington set the bounds of his realism early and moved comfortably within their amplitude for the remainder of his career. Although fellow novelist John Marquand remarked on this score as late as 1941, "He has proved that a man, if he is good enough, can keep up with the enormous variations of literary fashions,"[18] this remark represents the view of the minority. In the decades since Tarkington's death, when no aspect of subnormal, normal, or abnormal sexual relationship has not been exploited, the frankest works from Tarkington's pen seem mild indeed.

It might be remarked in passing that Tarkington shrewdly equated much of the mounting liberalism in fiction with the same motivation which often has been attributed to his own work, namely, money. To his perennial dismay, he noted that many a dramatic hit on Broadway and many a best-seller on the market depended largely upon the vulgarity of its sex and upon the crudity of its language to guarantee the popularity which also meant financial success. Tarkington's real quarrel in the issue was not over morality (although this cannot be dismissed); rather, it was over motivation. "An artist," Tarkington maintained, "will not suffer dirt; nor, though he may need and hope for reward, will he make anything with the mere motive of selling it."[19]

In the light of Tarkington's previous comments on the popular writer, we should slightly edit this pronouncement: in the clause "though he may need and hope for reward," we should insert *deserve*; and in the phrase "with the mere motive of selling it," we should underscore the word *mere*. Uncertain in Depression years about governmental subsidy for the artist, and unhappy in prosperous times about the gross profiteering of talent, Tarkington never wavered in his rejection of the salacious in art. He was aware that he might well incur both critical jibes from "the Sophisticates" for his "prudery" and derisive rebukes from a more liberal public for his conservatism; yet he stated his position in unequivocal terms. "A thing is not art if a pinch of dirt is deliberately added to it to make it sell," he declared. "That is to say, a thing may not be partly a work of art and partly dirt, though dirt may be cunningly and skillfully used to LOOK like a work of art."[20] Other adulterants are to be deplored as well, but the prostitution of art by the insertion of vulgarity he considered the cheapest.

### III   *The Author in the Marketplace*

It cannot be denied that Tarkington's refusal to keep step with the new liberalism in literature was a major factor in his critical demise. Fortunately for the Tarkington exchequer, at least, the greater part of his readership could not have cared less; and, even without "a pinch of dirt," his writings sold well. Most of his financial success he attributed to his skill as a professional writer. Whereas to many a literary critic the phrase "professional writer" is the apex of the uncomplimentary, Tarkington himself considered it a distinction. In 1939, shortly after his seventieth birthday, a *Life* magazine article by Charles Wertenbaker hailed Tarkington not only as "the dean of American letters" but also as "our No. 1 professional." To be placed topmost among the professionals might embarrass the man, but the novelist unquestionably was flattered. To Tarkington

the writer, the term carried connotations of skill, of craftsmanship, of artistry. The realistic practitioner once made the remark,
"Writing is a trade, and like any other trade, it must be learned."
The apprentice years of trial and error cannot be regarded
lightly, and the reading of popular taste is no mean skill.
As the result of his "professionalism," Tarkington was known
and beloved beyond any other author of his generation, and
he rejoiced in that distinction.

This insistence upon rapport with the general public may
suggest an inconsistency within the Tarkington literary complex.
On the one hand, he has been presented as "a gentleman"—
reared among genteel surroundings, educated amid Ivy League
traditions, and habituated to a life of culture. On the other
hand, the fact remains that Tarkington never lost his basic
trust in "the dear, good people." Under the protective tutelage
of a paternalistic capitalism, Tarkington had every confidence
in the ultimate integrity and taste of a cultivated citizenry.
Upon the death of James Whitcomb Riley, a fellow Hoosier
and a close family friend, Tarkington said in part, "The laurel
is bestowed by the people."[21] Some years later, when death
took Howells as well, Tarkington reiterated even more bluntly
his conviction that the reading public should be considered
the final arbiter in virtually all issues of literary taste. Sensitive
to the derogations which assaulted his long-time associate with
increasing frequency and vituperation, Tarkington warned
Howell's detractors, "In the long run, the people recommend
a work of art to the pompous critic; they sometimes take his
recommendations unaware that his pomposity is thus, after
all, a meekness."[22]

Not all persons hold Tarkington's opinion, by any means;
perhaps more prevalent is the conviction that it is "the passionate
few" rather than "the people" who preserve the finest in our
literary heritage. With respect to his own policy, however,
Tarkington deliberately ignored the reports which belittled the
broad reading public. Instead, as Charles Wertenbaker commented in the *Life* article, "Like all professionals, regardless
of private income, Tarkington has always written for the market.
. . . Being dependent on the public, or on editors who buy for
the public, he has tempered his writing to the taste of reason-

ably polite and intelligent people; but as a shrewd and honest observer of the people he writes for, he has mixed a good deal of sharp social criticism with his entertainment. Such a professional attitude often produces great literature, and Tarkington's best books have been praised by the best critics."[23] Like Charles Dickens before him, Tarkington was convinced that his primary responsibility as a novelist was to dramatize basic social truths in a style and form both comprehensible and palatable to a wide readership. Despite the handicaps of family, friends, and fortune, Tarkington remained, as Holliday put it, "very much like most people." In one of the warmest tributes one author could pay a fellow writer, John P. Marquand said of Tarkington at a still productive seventy-two, "By his own unvarying standards and good taste he has proved that literature can be produced outside of an ivory tower and sold in the market place."[24]

## IV  *The Shaping of a Writer*

Growing in grace as an author is not a process one can leave to chance. In his own way as confirmed an environmentalist as any within the Naturalist tradition, Tarkington placed primary stress upon the formative influences of the home. Long after he had put down his own roots and thrust out his own branches, it was evident that he had been a well-bent twig. The urbane atmosphere of "the new house," built when the boy was an impressionable six years old, was a constant resource for cultural growth and esthetic enjoyment. Even old age did not dim the memories of his mother playing "the great black grand piano near the bay window," of his father's library with "the same old rows of books on the same old polished brown shelves." Though rarely a snob, Tarkington was always a Brahmin. He was reared amid surroundings where beauty was a daily commodity, where culture was a cordial companion, and where courtesy was a pleasant friend. Given the same ingredients on the most modest scale, he was convinced, no one can fail to respond to such influences.

Although a loyal alumnus of Phillips Exeter Academy, Purdue, and Princeton, Tarkington remained a sturdy independent in

his attitudes toward the classroom as a "fertilizer from without."
Like many of his order, he held a dubious attitude toward
"writing courses." Even stylistic competence, he maintained, is
not a product of the classroom. "Writing must be learned, we
must serve our apprenticeship," he conceded; "but we must
work it out alone. There are no teachers. We must learn by
failure and repeated efforts how the thing is done."[25] As the
result of his perseverance, the Tarkington touch in matters of
style is probably his single talent upon which critics concur.
He himself had a final word of caution in this regard. "A master
craftsman is of course not necessarily an artist,"[26] he warned,
but the converse he would certainly also affirm.

At the same time, Tarkington was a staunch advocate of
academic experiences of a broad cultural nature for the embryo
writer. In general, he felt that a sound liberal arts program
was the finest preparation for "the more abundant life" of which
he spoke so often. Such a curriculum, he insisted, cannot help
but inculcate respect for the Western literary heritage and love
for the romance of words. Perhaps even higher than familiarity
with letters, Tarkington placed the study of history. At some
early point in an author's career, he was convinced, something
must awaken his social consciousness if he is going to pass
beyond the status of either the escapist or the dilettante. In
other words, any serious study by a novelist of consequence
should be permeated by what Tarkington called "a sense of
history." As he himself demonstrated in The Magnificent Ambersons, a good novel "carries more than its own weight." Beyond
all other considerations the writer should keep in mind the
socio-economic milieu out of which his story arises. In the
last analysis, the older Tarkington maintained, thematic substance contributes most to the formation of lasting letters.

Unfortunately for the critic, the mature Tarkington rarely
indulged in the role of literary arbiter. From such reluctance
to enter the lists, however, it should not be assumed that he
was a man of few convictions. Perhaps the most profound were
those concerning his concept of the serious writer and his role
in society. Once Tarkington himself realized the richness of
his Hoosier heritage, he returned to it again and again with
a sense of commitment which swept him through a long series

of studies on Midland America. As Alexander Black remarked in a 1922 Tarkington review entitled "What's in a Place?" "the real scene of every creative work is the heart of the novelist; nothing is real to him until he has found it there...."[27] Fundamental to the writer is a strong sense of identity with his subject which enables him to deal with it with sincerity and conviction.

Despite the proliferation of Tarkington's talents among adolescent idylls, summer romances, and comic interludes, there exists a fairly lofty plateau upon which the novelist sought to establish himself. Unhappy with many modern novels which he found "either 'highbrow' and unreadable or 'lowbrow' and not worth reading," Tarkington decided upon compromise. In effect he said, "There are highbrows and there are lowbrows; between them, however, is a goodly company of middlebrows to whom the writer can address his works. Let the novelist have the generosity to assume that his unknown public is of a kind to whom it is worth talking and for whom he should create the best of which he is capable." Never one to "write down" to any audience, Tarkington labored to maintain his course along the upper levels of stylistic excellence and thematic significance. "What kind of reader can a serious writer communicate with?" he once asked Kenneth Roberts. To his own question he replied, "He can fully communicate with those critical selves most like his own most critical self."[28]

In his late years, Tarkington sensed a growing disparity between "serious" and "popular" writing in modern literature. Suspicious of the "Sophisticates" and their cohorts among the "intelligentzia," Tarkington abjured the esoteric darlings of the academic world. In the same fashion he renounced the hack writers of cheap escape on the other end of the literary scale. Instead, Tarkington urged that the sincere novelist direct his work at the "upper-middlebrow" in a deliberate effort to raise popular taste. By so doing, Tarkington felt, the artist can play a constructive role in society rather than become a divisive influence. Equating the artist with the artisan in this regard, Tarkington stressed the need for the serious writer to rise above his own place and time in the building of a finer culture.

In this pursuit of stylistic quality the young author declared expansively, "We writers seek the finest, the most vivid means

of discovering and revealing things about life. We must make
our words into colors and sounds, and the cheap old tricks
and phrases won't do that. You've got to get living words out
of yourself. Nobody else's words; the used word is stale."[29]
Later, a wiser Tarkington blended words of caution with this
demand for originality. In particular, he admonished the writer
not to succumb to some current vogue which tends toward
mere novelty. "Fashion becomes a mob contagion," he warned;
"but at first, when the mob is small, we quicker parrots who
hop into it feel ourselves to be brilliantly superior, speaking a
language that is code to the vulgar." Such insistence upon
conformity to the cant of the moment Tarkington detected as
a temporary expedient leading only from one solution to another
problem. "When in time the mob grows enormous we remove
from it," he continued, "call it a rabble, despise its taste and
cackle of a new fashion, which may [well] be an old, old one
that we exclusives unwittingly revived."[30] Again, remarks like
these display the traditionalism which marks him as a writer;
but, as Charles Wertenbaker observed, "Booth Tarkington has too
much respect for the language not to treat it with deference."[31]

## V  Some Aspects of Style

Space does not permit extended analyses of passages from
the works of Tarkington which show his stylistic finesse, but a
few comments upon his verbal prowess are in order. His deft
touch in the sketching of word-portraits and his keen ear in the
cross-play of dialogue created descriptive drama in the depiction
of the commonplace. So familiar a phenomenon as a thunder-
storm assumes an almost poetic quality in the lyric sweep of
his figurative language; so homely a bit of Americana as the
front parlor takes on an aura of nostalgia in his evocative details.
His authentic descriptions duplicate the reader's own experiences;
his accurate settings partake of social history. Indeed, so aus-
picious is Tarkington's mastery of stylistic matters that reviewer
Clyde Beck was moved to remark, "There is the distinction of
the writer as opposed to the mere literary man. About such
prose clings the aroma of the classic. When a man writes with
such charm and flavor as Mr. Tarkington does nearly everywhere,

it is a safe conclusion that posterity will have something to say about him."[32] What substantives the future will provide for an equivocal "something," only time can tell.

Needless to say, Tarkington was a strong advocate of clarity in prose style. Although he often resorted to verbose circumlocutions for humorous effects in his lighter works (especially in the juveniles), he ordinarily employed a transparent, open style. Wherever the obscurantist appears in a Tarkington novel, his outré efforts were intended to lead only to ridicule. Tarkington held that communication is the first responsibility of the artist in any medium; hence, he insisted upon lucidity. In literature, the only bridge between author and reader is the written word, and Tarkington found scant justification for a writer's setting up barriers to obstruct his own purposes. Consequently, we search the Tarkington canon in vain for the contorted prose of a William Faulkner or for the involutions of a James Joyce.

For much the same reason, Tarkington resorted sparingly to the obliquities of symbolism in his writing. In *The Show Piece*, a sudden squall puts a trio of youngsters at the mercy of the sea; the incident, however, remains solely a device to reveal the egoism of Irvie Pease. "Dat ol' debbil sea" has no symbolic significance in the Eugene O'Neill sense, nor is it any cosmic force as with Herman Melville. Scattered details do have extended implications at rare intervals, but these are not abtruse by contemporary standards. In *The Midlander*, the falling of the cloud-shadow over Ornaby Addition certainly is imbued with prophetic import. In *Alice Adams*, the knot of violets, gathered at such cost by the girl, wilt and die at the dancing party quite as her summer hopes do. The building and demolition of the Amberson mansion in *The Magnificent Ambersons* surely symbolize the rise and fall of the family as well; and the union of George and Lucy is clearly a figurative merging of tradition and change. Throughout the other two novels in the *Growth* trilogy rises the most pervasive symbol in Tarkington fiction—the sooty plumes of industrial smoke. Even there, however, we sense more the limitations of the device in Tarkington's hands rather than its range. Although used more frequently than his detractors concede, the symbolism of Tarkington lacks the dimension and the intricacy which modern criticism prefers. Whether Tarkington himself would consider this a deficiency in his literary competence is open to question. Perhaps he realized that relatively few of his readers would recognize the subtleties of symbolism; in any case, he sacrificed cleverness for clarity.

In a similar vein, Tarkington took little issue with a problem that has vexed many a critic: the distinctions between a literature to "entertain" and a literature to "instruct." From the first, he placed a high premium upon the entertainment quality of his fiction. It was his conviction that even a reflective novel of social substance might well include the texture of plot and the color of romance if these factors will aid the author in "saying something" to his readers. In fact, he contended, any novel which fails to capture its reader by its narrative can never hold him by its abstract implications. Thus it is, as R. E. Banta observed of him at mid-career, "that the best of his efforts are important social documents, that the lightest of them have a Mark Twain quality of surviving freshness, and that they are all good entertainment."[33]

Closely akin to entertainment as a prime factor in fiction is humor. In the words of Tarkington, "comedy is, so far, the only alleviation of life, except work and what is called faith. I should call it the third best thing in life."[34] As a matter of fact, he went, upon occasion, so far as to rank comedy above tragedy, both in its composition and its function. Quite aware of the lowly position of the comic element within critical circles, Tarkington himself accorded humor a high respect and devoted to it the same artistry with which he treated serious subjects. In a conversation with Kenneth Roberts at mid-career, he insisted that "a writer who is sincerely, and often in a humorous manner, engaged in the interpretation of life doesn't edit his writing with the idea that he's offering entertainment, no matter if he be by nature and in manner a humorist." The finest effect in all literature, he added, is "a pathos which only a master craftsman can attain ... tears, not of sorrow, but of delight."[35]

In regard to Tarkington's avoiding the extremes of Romanticism and Naturalism, Arthur H. Quinn said, "it was Booth Tarkington's sense of humor that saved him from both dangers."[36]

Let it be said also, however, that this same sense of humor has been a persistent stumbling block in academic appraisals of him. E. B. White said truly, "The world likes humor, but it treats it patronizingly. It decorates its serious writers with laurel, and its wags with Brussels sprouts."[37] With Tarkington, there is some justification for critical complaint, for he did resort to humor upon occasion as an easy way out of painful situations. As "the third best thing in life," it may indeed function as a vital stabilizing factor amid the adversities of life; it also may emerge as grotesquery when used under false pretenses.

## VI  *A Creed for the Future*

Perhaps the best explanation for these occasional lapses in comic judgment is Tarkington's indomitable optimism. The reader should recall that the national crises of the last decade and a half of his career might well have overwhelmed a less resilient spirit. Although the Depression did not affect his own scale of living, he was deeply concerned about the debilitating effects of prolonged economic distress upon the national temper. Dismayed by the Socialist tendencies of the Roosevelt administration and by the leftist movements in every direction, he campaigned vigorously with his pen to preserve the American heritage of enlightened democracy. When the situation abroad threatened a second world war within his adult years, he stood firm for "peace at all costs." And finally, when that warfare again rocked the world, he rallied to the Allied cause with propaganda pieces commissioned by the government, personal appearances on bond drives, and a round of fiction on patriotic themes.

Although banished in his last years to critical exile, Tarkington never lost hope that American letters might experience "a return to curative writers." Indeed, amid the vagaries of a world tensed for "future shock," he felt that there now rests upon authors in general a grave obligation to assist in restoring the dignity of the human spirit. In Tarkington terms, an aging Van Wyck Brooks declared in *The Writer in America* (1953), "we need above all at present those who can restore for us a feeling for the true aims of living, who can remind us of the goodness in men, bring back the joy of life and give one a

sense of hope."[38] Here Brooks supplies most of the planks for
Tarkington's literary platform. To the last, Tarkington maintained that it is the duty of the responsible novelist to make
his reader feel "full of courage and the capacity for happiness
in a brightened world." Amid the perplexities of the everyday,
he was aware that "there are fewer tears of joy than sorrow";
hence his justification in the domain of fiction for a dash of
romance, touches of humor, moments of nostalgia. Whatever
his method, Tarkington felt the sincere writer can perform no
higher service than "to lift the human spirit." More than a molder
of public opinion, more than a mover of public action, the true
artist is the maker of man in the highest sense.

We might argue that with Tarkington something vanished
from our American "way of life," something which would stand
us in good stead in a none-too-brave new world. Shortly after
the death of the novelist, while conducting extensive research for
an early study on Tarkington, Carl Bennett called upon the
editor of a magazine which had published much of Tarkington's
fiction. "At the mention of Tarkington's name, he exclaimed,
'May God rest his soul—he was the last American!' "[39] What
prompted this outburst involves a major portion of this study,
for Tarkington did personify much in the traditional American
national character. Basic in the man were his philosophy of
individualism, his faith in democratic order, his emphasis upon
the gospel of work, and, above all, his confidence in the abundant
promise of America. With all its flaws, Tarkington also placed
explicit trust in paternalistic capitalism as the best socio-economic
structure thus far devised by man and peculiar in its purest
form to the United States. Under its aegis, he prophesied that
mankind would reach its highest level of achievment in every
field of human endeavor.

Supremely important for Tarkington in "the American way
of life" is the preeminence of the individual; for him, the state
exists for man, instead of man's existing for the state. Notwithstanding his esthetic proclivities, Tarkington urged the
primacy of man. "To us [the artists]," he made clear, "there is
one thing more important than art, and that is life."[40] In a
companion comment reflecting his basic humanism, Tarkington
declared, "Mankind's most important affair is to discover what

life itself is, why it exists and therefore where it is going. . . . Whoever makes more comprehensible a part of life has helped that much, even if infinitesimally, toward the answer to the question ever within the consciousness of us all."[41] Although Tarkington was an ardent advocate of technological advancement in an industrial age, he beheld with dismay "the lopsided progress . . . of scientific material advance achieved by nations underdeveloped in spirit."[42] In terms increasingly familiar since his time, Tarkington deplored the dehumanizing aspects of an industrialized society, and called for the reemergence of man on a truly personal plane. Tarkington felt that an American literature of power should dramatize "the inalienable rights" and "the inviolable individuality" of every citizen in a unique society.

In the main, he called for a fresh appraisal of the American character and a new esteem for the nation's cultural potential. From his travels abroad, he realized that "the European and British tradition that America is the land of the Almighty Dollar, and of no culture, still prevails abroad, not only among the unlearned and untraveled, but also among the sophisticated."[43] Comparing the stereotypes of the American national culture to the stock figures of catchpenny novels, Tarkington protested that "We are less simple and infinitely less of a pattern than foreigners suppose, and no one is in a better position to portray the true American than the perceptive word-artist."[44] In the tradition of Irving and Emerson a century before him, Tarkington called for a revitalized national literature honest to the virtues of the country it portrayed.

With typical optimism, Tarkington surveyed the literary scene in his last years and declared that "the revolution has begun." Drawing upon its native dynamism and the impetus of World War II, the United States seemed headed for new heights of artistic creativity. To Tarkington, even the nation's relative youth was an asset, for it should breed an active curiosity, a healthy competitive spirit, and a constructive courage. He wrote at that time, "A living and growing culture, eager to discern and appreciate the kinds of culture other than its own, has the vigor and generosity that will keep it from self-worship; for self-worship means stagnation. American culture is still moving, and more than ever appreciative of other culture; it has not crystallized into rigidity or turned back upon itself to become decadent. It lives and is safe even from its defenders."[45] In the world of letters, indeed, of the arts in general, Tarkington looked for the artisans of the New World to shape a whole new chapter in the continuum of culture.

## VII  A Legacy Adrift

The "summing up" of Newton Booth Tarkington presents unusual problems for the critic. As the winner of important literary awards and the recipient of prestigious academic distinctions, he must be accorded proper deference. As the author of over thirty novels, a prodigious quantity of short stories, and a sizable number of successful plays, he is a penman of considerable accomplishment. As the subject of frequent biographical and critical studies during a long career, he is an artist of recognized stature. What, then, are the problems?

In general terms, the problems concerning the fictional writing of Tarkington consist of an overall unevenness in quality, sporadic lapses into melodrama or sentimentality, a seemingly casual treatment of primary issues, and an excessive reliance upon simplistic solutions. Tarkington himself has been accused of neglecting the consequential, evading the provocative, and avoiding the controversial; likewise, he has been charged with pandering to popular taste, with failing to "grow up" and "toughen up," as well as with holding himself aloof from the currents of change.

The inescapable truth is that Tarkington retained a relative conservatism during a period of dramatic liberalization. Despite the quantity of his literary output, Tarkington never really "wrote himself out"; for current criticism, he simply wrote too much in much the same ways. Nearly two decades before his death he admitted that the "ultra-moderns" probably considered him "a complacent old gentleman," and he was no doubt right about their opinions. Under similar circumstances a latter-day Howells wrote Mark Twain, "I feel myself a very tiresome old story." Such a plaint smacks strongly of weariness, of self-pity, of resignation; but these terms are not found in the Tarkington lexicon. Composing steadily until his death on May 19, 1946, he remained faithful to the literary principles of a selective Realism which he had inherited from the past and which he hoped might be his legacy for the future.

In *The Enchanted Glass* (1936), Hardin Craig observes, "If, in general, the writer falls in with the best or even with the most widely held opinions of his time, he will, if his art is adequate, be what is called popular. If his thought has currency after he is dead, he will live on in literature."[46] With its dual emphasis upon "art" and "thought," this remark holds special meaning for Tarkington; in *Some Old Portraits*, he too asserts that "the 'how' and the 'what' are inseparable elements in an artist's significance."[47] Posterity may ignore many of his individual works; but the further one penetrates into the Tarkington concept of literature and its role in society, the more willingly he concedes the man a worthy position in our national letters.

# Notes and References

## Preface

1. Van Wyck Brooks, *The Writer in America* (New York, 1953), pp. 40-41.
2. Booth Tarkington, *Some Old Portraits* (New York, 1939), p. 206.

## Chapter One

1. Bernard De Voto, "The American Scholar," *Minority Report* (Boston, 1940), p. 345.
2. James Woodress, *Booth Tarkington: Gentleman from Indiana* (New York, 1954), p. 7.
3. John P. Marquand, "Tarkington and Social Significance," *Saturday Review of Literature*, XXIII (March 1, 1941), 7.
4. E. S. Martin, "And How!" *Saturday Review of Literature*, V (November 24, 1928), 396.
5. Woodress, *Booth Tarkington*, p. 22.
6. *Ibid.*, p. 23.
7. *Ibid.*, p. 31.
8. *Ibid.*, p. 32.
9. Malcolm Cowley, "How Writers Write," *Saturday Review*, XL (November 30, 1957), 11.
10. Woodress, *Booth Tarkington*, p. 53.
11. *Ibid.*, p. 56.
12. *Ibid.*, p. 58.

## Chapter Two

1. J. Isaacs, *An Assessment of Twentieth-Century Literature* (London, 1951), p. 21.
2. Bernard DeVoto, "From Dream to Fiction," *Minority Report* (Boston, 1940), p. 220.
3. Henry Steele Commager, "The Rise of the City," *Senior Scholastic*, LVI (May 10, 1950), 13.
4. Robert Coates Holliday, "Tarkingtonapolis," *Broome Street Straws* (New York, 1919), p. 169.

5. Meredith Nicholson, "Let Main Street Alone!" *The Provincial American and Other Papers* (Boston, 1912), p. 15.

6. J. Donald Adams, *The Shape of Books to Come* (New York, 1944), p. 4.

7. Tarkington, *The Midlanders* (Garden City, N.Y., 1924), Seawood Edition, Volume XVIII, p. 404.

8. Tarkington, *Mr. White, The Red Barn, Hell and Bridgewater* (Garden City, N.Y., 1935), p. xiii.

9. *Ibid.*, p. xvi.

10. *Ibid.*, p. xvii.

11. Maxwell Geismar, *Rebels and Ancestors: The American Novel, 1890-1915* (Cambridge, Mass., 1953), p. 383.

12. Irwin Edman, "Patterns for the Free," *Adam, The Baby and the Man from Mars* (Cambridge, Mass., 1929), p. 145.

13. Tarkington, *Some Old Portraits*, p. 203.

14. Willard Thorp, *American Writing in the Twentieth Century* (Cambridge, Mass., 1960), p. 145.

15. *Ibid.*, p. 183.

16. Philip Rahv, "Notes on the Decline of Naturalism," *Image and Idea* (New York, 1949), p. 134.

17. Woodress, *Booth Tarkington*, p. 60.

18. Tarkington, "Let Us Confound Them," *Saturday Review of Literature*, XXXIX (April 20, 1929), 899.

19. Walter W. Schmauch, *Christmas Literature through the Centuries* (Chicago, 1938), p. 298.

20. Woodress, *Booth Tarkington*, p. 68.

21. *Ibid.*, pp. 71-72.

22. Fred Lewis Pattee, *The Development of the American Short Story* (New York, 1923), p. 369.

23. Tarkington, quoted by Woodress, *Booth Tarkington*, p. 87.

24. F. O. Matthiessen, *Sarah Orne Jewett* (Cambridge, Mass., 1929), pp. 110-11.

25. Woodress, *Booth Tarkington*, p. 83.

26. Frederick L. Allen, "Best-Sellers: 1900-1935," *Saturday Review of Literature*, XIII (December 7, 1935), 3-4.

27. Woodress, *Booth Tarkington*, p. 74.

## Chapter Three

1. Tarkington, quoted by Woodress, *Booth Tarkington*, pp. 74-75.

2. Hamlin Garland, *Crumbling Idols* (Cambridge, Mass., 1960), p. 30.

3. Woodress, *Booth Tarkington*, p. 75.

4. Barton Currie, "An Editor in Pursuit of Booth Tarkington," *Princeton University Chronicle*, XVI (Winter 1955), 81.

5. Tarkington, Letter to parents, February 1, 1899, *Princeton University Chronicle*, XVI (Winter 1955), 56.

6. *Ibid.*

7. *Ibid.*, p. 60.

8. *Ibid.*, p. 61.

9. James Woodress, "Tarkington's New York Literary Debut," *Princeton University Chronicle*, XVI (Winter 1955), 79.

10. Woodress, *Booth Tarkington*, p. 82.

11. Tarkington, *Some Old Portraits*, p. x.

12. Woodress, *Booth Tarkington*, p. 19.

13. Tarkington, "As I Seem to Me," *Saturday Evening Post*, CCXIV (August 2, 1941), 44.

14. Tarkington, "Mr. Howells," *Harper's Magazine*, CXLI (August 1920), 346.

15. Woodress, "Debut," p. 46.

16. Tarkington, *Some Old Portraits*, p. 204.

17. Tarkington, "Mr. Howells," p. 350.

18. Woodress, *Booth Tarkington*, p. 16.

19. Tarkington, quoted by Woodress, *Booth Tarkington*, p. 187.

20. Tarkington, "Mr. Howells," p. 350.

21. Tarkington, "Appreciation of the Author," *The Name of Old Glory*, ed. by James Whitcomb Riley (Indianapolis, 1917), p. 19.

22. Tarkington, *Some Old Portraits*, p. 45.

23. Woodress, *Booth Tarkington*, pp. 187-88.

24. *Ibid.*, p. 64.

25. *Ibid.*, p. 92.

26. Tarkington, Letter to Dan Calkins, The Tarkington Papers, Princeton University Library.

27. Woodress, *Booth Tarkington*, p. 127.

28. Tarkington, Letter to Judge Tarkington, Papers.

29. Woodress, *Booth Tarkington*, p. 156.

30. *Ibid.*, p. 163.

31. Tarkington, quoted by Woodress, *Booth Tarkington*, p. 165.

32. Tarkington, "Nipskillions," *Looking Forward and Others* (New York, 1926), p. 27.

## Chapter Four

1. Woodress, *Booth Tarkington*, p. 181.

2. Tarkington, Letter to unnamed friend, Tarkington Papers, Princeton University Library.

3. Tarkington, *The Turmoil* (New York, 1915), p. 201.

4. Woodress, *Booth Tarkington,* p. 445.

5. Tarkington, *The Turmoil,* p. 231.

6. *Ibid.,* p. 319.

7. R. Ellis Roberts, "Mr. Tarkington Through British Eyes," *Living Age,* CCC (March 1, 1919), 544.

8. Tarkington, "Rotarian and Sophisticate," *World's Work,* LVIII (January 1929), 43.

9. Tarkington, "America and Culture," *Saturday Evening Post,* CCI (March 2, 1929), 25.

10. Paul Meadows, *The Culture of Industrial Man* (Lincoln, Neb., 1950), p. 117.

11. Tarkington, "Rotarian and Sophisticate," p. 43.

12. Mark Schorer, *Sinclair Lewis: An American Life* (New York, 1961), p. 356.

13. *Ibid.*

14. Woodress, *Booth Tarkington,* p. 183.

15. Tarkington, *The Turmoil,* p. 6.

16. *Ibid.,* pp. 6-7.

17. *Ibid.,* pp. 1-2.

18. Tarkington, *The Magnificent Ambersons* (New York, 1918), p. 272.

19. *Ibid.*

20. *Ibid.,* p. 273.

21. *Ibid.,* p. 475.

22. Tarkington, *The Midlander,* p. 435.

23. *Ibid.,* p. 347.

24. *Ibid.,* p. 348.

25. *Ibid.,* p. 492.

26. Henry Seidel Canby, *The Age of Confidence* (New York, 1934), p. 232.

27. Woodress, *Booth Tarkington,* p. 265.

28. Tarkington, *The Plutocrat* (Garden City, N.Y., 1927), p. 462.

29. *Ibid.,* p. 463.

30. Woodress, *Booth Tarkington,* p. 266.

31. Tarkington, quoted by Woodress, *Booth Tarkington,* p. 266.

32. Harold Murray, quoted by Woodress, *Booth Tarkington,* p. 307.

33. Marquand, *op. cit.,* p. 70.

34. Woodress, *Booth Tarkington,* p. 308.

35. *Ibid.,* p. 408.

36. Marquand, *op. cit.,* p. 7.

## Chapter Five

1. Robert S. and Helen M. Lynd, *Middletown: A Study in Contemporary American Culture* (New York, 1929), p. 231.

2. William Dean Howells, "Realism and the American Novel," *Criticism and Fiction* (Cambridge, Mass., 1962 reprint), p. 149.

3. Tarkington, quoted by Kenneth Roberts, "A Gentleman from Maine and Indiana," *Saturday Evening Post*, CCIV (August 8, 1931), 57.

4. Thomas Beer, *The Mauve Decade: American Life at the End of the Nineteenth Century* (New York, 1954), p. 18.

5. *Ibid.*, p. 161.

6. Edith Wharton, *A Backward Glance* (New York, 1934), pp. 139-40.

7. Robert Coates Holliday, *Booth Tarkington* (New York, 1918), p. 141.

8. Tarkington, *The Flirt* (New York, 1913), pp. 71-72.

9. Quinn, *op. cit.*, p. 600.

10. Woodress, *Booth Tarkington*, p. 169.

11. Tarkington, *Alice Adams* (New York, 1921), Signet Edition, p. 232.

12. Anonymous, "Another Mainstreet," *The Literary Digest*, LXX (July 23, 1921), 44.

13. Ellen Glasgow, Letter quoted by Woodress in *Booth Tarkington*, pp. 249-50.

14. Sinclair Lewis, Letter to Tarkington (1921), Mark Schorer, *op. cit.*, p. 304.

15. Tarkington, *The Show Piece* (Garden City, N.Y., 1947), p. ix.

16. *Ibid.*

17. *Ibid.*, pp. viii-ix.

18. *Ibid.*, p. ix.

19. *Ibid.*

20. Carl Van Doren, "The Parasite's Tragedy," *Nation*, CXIII (August 3, 1921), 125.

21. Edith Wyatt, "Booth Tarkington: The Seven Ages of Man," *North American Review*, CCXVI (October 1922), 510.

22. Quinn, *op. cit.*, p. 603.

23. Joseph Collins, "The New Mr. Tarkington," *Bookman*, LXV (March 1927), 19.

24. Tarkington, *Claire Ambler* (Garden City, N.Y., 1928), p. 73.

25. Tarkington, *Some Old Portraits* (New York, 1939), p. 108.

26. Tarkington, *Kate Fennigate* (Garden City, N.Y., 1943), pp. 34-35.

27. Hjalmer H. Boyesen, "Types of American Women," *Literary and Social Silhouettes* (New York, 1894), p. 18.

28. R. E. Banta, *Indiana Authors and Their Books* (Crawfordsville, Ind., 1949), p. 313.

29. Carl D. Bennett, "Faculty Studies: A Report on Wesleyan's Participation in a Five-Year Program of Grants," *Wesleyan College Bulletin*, XXXIII (May 1952), 6.

30. James Woodress, "The Tarkington Papers," *Princeton University Library Bulletin*, XVI (Winter 1955), 46.

31. Collins, *op. cit.*, p. 19.

32. Michael Millgate, *American Social Fiction: James to Cozzens* (New York, 1967), p. 71.

33. Tarkington, *The Plutocrat* (Garden City, N.Y., 1927), p. 543.

34. Millgate, *op. cit.*, p. 71.

35. *Ibid.*, p. 69.

36. Woodress, *Booth Tarkington*, p. 257.

## Chapter Six

1. Woodress, *Booth Tarkington*, p. 174.

2. Tarkington, quoted by Woodress, *Booth Tarkington*, p. 174.

3. Tarkington, "The Golden Age," *Looking Forward and Others* (Garden City, N.Y., 1926), pp. 137-38.

4. Tarkington, "As I Seem to Me," *Saturday Evening Post*, CCXVI (August 16, 1941), 48.

5. Tarkington, "The Golden Age," p. 136.

6. Tarkington, "What I Have Learned from Boys," *American Magazine*, XCIX (January 1925), 5.

7. *Ibid.*, p. 6.

8. *Ibid.*, p. 5.

9. Carl Van Doren, *Contemporary American Novelists* (New York, 1922), p. 87.

10. Fred Lewis Pattee, *The New American Literature, 1890-1930* (New York, 1930), pp. 77-78.

11. Grant C. Knight, *American Literature and Culture* (New York, 1932), p. 430.

12. Tarkington, *Penrod: His Complete Story* (Garden City, N.Y., 1946), p. 36.

13. *Ibid.*, p. 39.

14. Van Wyck Brooks, *Writer in America*, p. 64.

15. Van Doren, *Contemporary American Novelists*, p. 87.

16. James Branch Cabell, *Beyond Life* (New York, 1921), p. 307.

17. Grant Overton, *Authors of Our Day: Studies in Contemporary Literature* (New York, 1924), p. 121.

18. Edith F. Wyatt, "Booth Tarkington: The Seven Ages of Man," *North American Review*, CCXVI (October 1922), 500.

19. Robert Holliday, *Booth Tarkington*, p. 170.

20. William Lyon Phelps, ed., *Whilomville Stories* by Stephen Crane (New York, 1926), p. xi.

21. Woodress, *Booth Tarkington*, p. 176.

22. Richard Crowley, "Booth Tarkington: Time for Revival," *America*, XC (February 13, 1954), 509.

23. Woodress, *Booth Tarkington*, p. 166.

24. *Ibid.*, p. 173.

25. Tarkington, Letter to Julian Street, quoted by Woodress, *Booth Tarkington*, pp. 179-80.

26. Tarkington, quoted by Woodress, *Booth Tarkington*, p. 179.

27. *Ibid.*, p. 178.

28. *Ibid.*, p. 177.

29. Tarkington, "The Golden Age," p. 125.

30. Elmer C. Adams, "Mr. Tarkington Reverts to the Playful Manner," Detroit *News* (May 7, 1922), 14.

31. *Ibid.*

32. Tarkington, *Penrod: His Complete Story*, p. 48.

33. *Ibid.*, p. 49.

34. Tarkington, *Seventeen* (New York, 1917), p. 12.

35. Tarkington, *Gentle Julia* (Garden City, N.Y., 1922), pp. 84-85.

36. Tarkington, *Seventeen*, p. 325.

37. Woodress, *Booth Tarkington*, p. 192.

*Chapter Seven*

1. Tarkington, Letter to George Tyler, quoted by Woodress, *Booth Tarkington*, p. 255.

2. *Ibid.*, p. 256.

3. Tarkington, *The Midlander*, p. 486.

4. Woodress, *Booth Tarkington*, p. 256.

5. *Ibid.*, p. 280.

6. Tarkington, "High Summer," quoted by Woodress, *Booth Tarkington*, p. 280.

7. E. S. Martin, *op. cit.*, p. 396.

8. Maxwell Geismar, *Rebels and Ancestors: The American Novel, 1890-1915* (Cambridge, Mass., 1953), p. 383.

9. Tarkington, *Some Old Portraits*, p. 203.

10. *Ibid.*, p. 204.

11. Tarkington, quoted by David Karsner, *Sixteen Authors to One* (New York, 1928), pp. 92-93.

12. Tarkington, *The Flirt*, p. 340.

13. Tarkington, quoted by Kenneth Roberts, "The Gentleman from Maine and Indiana," *Saturday Evening Post*, CCIV (August 8, 1931), 57.

14. Tarkington, "When Is It Dirt?" *Collier's*, LXXIX (May 14, 1927), 8.

15. Tarkington, quoted by Karsner, *op. cit.*, p. 92.

16. Tarkington, quoted by S. J. Woolf in "The Gentleman from Indiana at 70," *New York Times Magazine* (July 23, 1939), 15.

17. Bennett, *op. cit.*, p. 90.

18. Marquand, *op. cit.*, p. 7.

19. Tarkington, "When Is It Dirt?" 98.

20. *Ibid.*

21. Tarkington, "Mr. Riley," *Collier's Weekly*, LVIII (December 30, 1916), 17.

22. Tarkington, "Mr. Howells," *Harper's Magazine*, CXLI (August 1920), 346.

23. Charles Wertenbaker, "Booth Tarkington," *Life*, VII (September 4, 1939), 55.

24. Marquand, *op. cit.*, p. 7.

25. Tarkington, quoted by Asa Dickinson in *Booth Tarkington* (Garden City, N.Y., n.d.), p. 4.

26. Tarkington, *Some Old Portraits*, p. 38.

27. Alexander Black, "What's In a Place?" *The Latest Thing and Other Things* (New York, 1922), p. 210.

28. Tarkington, quoted by Kenneth Roberts, *op. cit.*, p. 57.

29. Tarkington, quoted by David Karsner, *op. cit.*, p. 93.

30. Tarkington, *Some Old Portraits*, p. 104.

31. Wertenbaker, *op. cit.*, p. 55.

32. Clyde Beck, "Tarkington as a Master of Literary Composition," *Detroit News* (November 11, 1932).

33. R. E. Banta, *Indiana Authors and Their Books*, p. 318.

34. Tarkington, "Nipskillions," *Looking Forward and Others* (Garden City, N.Y., 1926), p. 36.

35. Tarkington, quoted by Woodress, *Booth Tarkington*, p. 85.

36. Quinn, *op. cit.*, p. 596.

37. E. B. White, *A Subtreasury of American Humor*, ed. with Katharine S. White (New York, 1941), p. xviii.

38. Van Wyck Brooks, *The Writer in America*, p. 189.

39. Carl Bennett, "Faculty Studies: A Report on Wesleyan's

Participation in a Five-Year Program of Grants," *Wesleyan College Bulletin*, XXXIII (May 1952), 6.

40. Tarkington, *Some Old Portraits*, p. xiii.

41. *Ibid.*, pp. xii-xiii.

42. Tarkington, "What of the Night?" *Good Housekeeping*, CXVIII (May 1944), 17.

43. Tarkington, "America and Culture," *Saturday Evening Post*, CCI (March 2, 1929), 25.

44. *Ibid.*, p. 120.

45. Tarkington, "America and Culture," p. 120.

46. Hardin Craig, *The Enchanted Glass* (New York, 1939), p. 83.

47. Tarkington, *Some Old Portraits*, p. 206.

# Selected Bibliography

Those who wish to make further study of Tarkington and his writings should first consult "The Literary Development of Booth Tarkington," an unpublished manuscript by Carl D. Bennett (Emory University, 1954). Touching upon all phases of Tarkington's works, this critical analysis presents an excellent overview of his career in letters. For a delightful blend of biography and criticism, *Booth Tarkington: Gentleman from Indiana* by James Woodress has no peer. Utilizing for the first time the Tarkington Papers at Princeton University and many resources among Tarkington's family and associates, Woodress adds fresh, new dimensions to the Hoosier novelist.

The collection at Princeton is described in some detail by Woodress in an article titled "The Tarkington Papers" (*The Princeton University Library Chronicle*, XVI, 2 [Winter 1955]). The same issue includes Barton Currie's warm tribute to Tarkington, "An Editor in Pursuit of Booth Tarkington," a sampling of Tarkington's letters "back home" while the young author was in New York City preparing *The Gentleman from Indiana* for serialization, and an extended listing of fugitive pieces by Tarkington.

These last items in the *Chronicle* are additions to *A Bibliography of Booth Tarkington*, the primary resource for Tarkington publications. Prompted by the death of the novelist in 1946, this descriptive bibliography is a compendious catalogue co-edited by Dorothy R. Russo and Thelma L. Sullivan and published by the Indiana Historical Society in 1949. Its rare omissions are more than compensated for by its convenient format and scrupulous detail.

PRIMARY SOURCES

1. Novels (complete)

*Alice Adams.* New York: Grosset and Dunlap, 1921.
*Beasley's Christmas Party.* New York: Harper and Brothers, 1909.
*The Beautiful Lady.* New York: McClure, Phillips and Co., 1905.
*Beauty and the Jacobin.* New York: Harper and Brothers, 1912.
*Cherry.* New York: Harper and Brothers, 1903.
*Claire Ambler.* Garden City, N.Y.: Doubleday, Doran and Co., 1928.

*The Conquest of Canaan.* New York: Harper and Brothers, 1905.

*The Fighting Littles.* Garden City, N.Y.: Doubleday, Doran and Co., 1941.

*The Flirt.* Garden City, N.Y.: Doubleday, Page and Co., 1913.

*Gentle Julia.* Garden City, N.Y.: Doubleday, Page and Co., 1922.

*The Gentleman from Indiana.* New York: Doubleday and McClure Company, 1899.

*The Guest of Quesnay.* New York: The McClure Co., 1908.

*The Heritage of Hatcher Ide.* Garden City, N.Y.: Doubleday, Doran and Co., 1941.

*His Own People.* Garden City, N.Y.: Doubleday, Page and Co., 1907.

*Image of Josephine.* Garden City, N.Y.: Doubleday, Doran and Co., 1945.

*Kate Fennigate.* Garden City, N.Y.: Doubleday, Doran and Co., 1943.

*Little Orvie.* Garden City, N.Y.: Doubleday, Doran and Co., 1934.

*The Lorenzo Bunch.* Garden City, N.Y.: Doubleday, Doran and Co., 1936.

*The Magnificent Ambersons.* Garden City, N.Y.: Doubleday, Page and Company, 1918.

*Mary's Neck.* Garden City, N.Y.: Doubleday, Doran and Co., 1932.

*The Midlander.* Garden City, N.Y.: Doubleday, Page and Co., 1924.

*Mirthful Haven.* Garden City, N.Y.: Doubleday, Doran and Co., 1930.

*Monsieur Beaucaire.* New York: McClure, Phillips and Co., 1900.

*Penrod: His Complete Story* (consisting of *Penrod, Penrod and Sam,* and *Penrod Jashber;* Preface by the author). Garden City, N.Y.: Doubleday, Doran and Co., 1946.

*The Plutocrat.* Garden City, N.Y.: Doubleday, Page and Co., 1927.

*Presenting Lily Mars.* Garden City, N.Y.: Doubleday, Doran and Co., 1933.

*Ramsey Milholland.* Garden City, N.Y.: Doubleday, Page and Co., 1919.

*Rumbin Galleries.* New York: The Literary Guild of America, 1937.

*Seventeen.* New York: Harper and Brothers, 1916.

*The Show Piece.* Garden City, N.Y.: Doubleday and Co., 1947.

*Three Selected Short Novels.* Garden City, N.Y.: Doubleday and Co., 1947.

*The Turmoil.* New York: Harper and Brothers, 1915.

*The Two Vanrevels.* New York: McClure, Phillips and Co., 1902.

*Wanton Mally.* Garden City, N.Y.: Doubleday, Doran and Co., 1932.

*Women.* Garden City, N.Y.: Doubleday, Page and Co., 1925.

*Young Mrs. Greeley.* Garden City, N.Y.: Doubleday, Doran and Co., 1929.

2. Selected Articles, Short Stories, and Miscellaneous Prose Works

"As I Seem to Me." *Saturday Evening Post,* CCXIV (July 5-August 23, 1941).
*Looking Forward and Others.* Garden City, N.Y.: Doubleday, Page and Co., 1926.
"The Middle West." *Harper's Monthly Magazine,* CVI (December 1902), 75-83.
"Mr. Howells." *Harper's Magazine,* CXLI (August 1920), 346-50.
*Mr. White, The Red Barn, Hell and Bridgewater.* Garden City, N.Y.: Doubleday, Doran and Company, 1935.
"Rotarian and Sophisticate." *World's Work,* LVIII (January 1929), 42-44+.
*Some Old Portraits.* Garden City, N.Y.: Doubleday, Doran and Co., 1939.
*The World Does Move.* Garden City, N.Y.: Doubleday, Doran and Company, 1928.
"What I Have Learned from Boys." *American Magazine,* XCIX (January 1925), 5-7+.
"When Is It Dirt?" *Collier's,* LXXIX (May 14, 1927), 8-9.

SECONDARY SOURCES

BANTA, R. E. *Indiana Authors and Their Books* (1816-1916). Crawfordsville, Indiana: Wabash College, 1949. Brief but sympathetic glance at Tarkington in his formative years.
BENNETT, CARL D. *The Literary Development of Booth Tarkington.* Unpublished Ph.D. Dissertation, Emory University, 1944. Most useful survey of the man and his works; includes a fine set of secondary resources.
BOYNTON, H. W. "All Sorts," *Bookman,* XLVIII (December 1918), 489-95. Early acknowledgment of Tarkington's talents in a wide range of subjects and styles.
COLLINS, JOSEPH. "The New Mr. Tarkington," *Bookman,* LXV (March 1927), 12-21. Good contemporary account of Tarkington's rise in critical esteem after the completion of the *Growth* trilogy.
CROWLEY, RICHARD. "Booth Tarkington: Time for Revival." *America,* XC (February 13, 1954), 508-10. Persuasive alignment of arguments for a reappraisal of Tarkington; contains cogent comments on his critical neglect. Provocative.
CURRIE, BARTON. "An Editor in Pursuit of Booth Tarkington." *Princeton University Library Chronicle,* XVI (Winter 1955), 80-88. Illuminating comments upon Tarkington the man by a long-time friend, editor, and bibliophile. Spirited defense.

DICKINSON, ASA D. *Booth Tarkington*. Garden City, N.Y.: Doubleday, Page and Company, no date. Still a useful critical biography of mid-career Tarkington. Somewhat overdrawn, yet rich in fugitive details.

HANSEN, HARRY. *Midwest Portraits*. New York: Harcourt, Brace and Company, 1923. Abbreviated in every respect, yet perceptive in its estimate of Tarkington in his peak years.

HOLLIDAY, ROBERT C. *Booth Tarkington*. New York: Doubleday, Page and Company, 1918. Strictly a professional job for Tarkington's own publisher. Though an early work, a good resource for biographical details of those exploratory years.

KARSNER, DAVID. *Sixteen Authors to One*. New York: Lewis Copeland Company, 1928. Highly journalistic work of interest mainly because of its use of personal interviews.

KRUTCH, JOSEPH WOOD. "Crowned by the Booster's Club." *Nation*, CXVIII (March 19, 1924), 318-19. Though largely a cordial tribute to *The Midlander*, this article suggests several aspects of Tarkington as serious social critic.

MARQUAND, JOHN P. "Tarkington and Social Significance," *Saturday Review of Literature*, XXIII (March 1, 1941), 7. Brief but discerning commentary on Tarkington's persistent concern for single man in a multiple society.

NICHOLSON, MEREDITH. *The Hoosiers*. New York: The Macmillan Company, 1916. Fine contemporary history of the Hoosier School in general, with helpful details on personal interrelationships within the group. Tarkington fares well.

ROBERTS, KENNETH. "A Gentleman from Maine and Indiana." *Saturday Evening Post*, CCIV (August 8, 1931), 14-15+. Highly personal account of friendship between Tarkington and the younger author. Comments on writers and writing of most use.

RUSSO, DOROTHY R. and THELMA L. SULLIVAN. *A Bibliography of Booth Tarkington*, 1869-1946. Indianapolis: Indianapolis Historical Society, Lakeside Press, 1949. Indispensable descriptive catalogue of nearly all Tarkington items in print. A must for primary resources.

RUSSO, DOROTHY R. *et al.* "Additions to the Tarkington Bibliography." Princeton University Library *Chronicle*, XVI (Winter 1955), 89-94. Actually a supplement of miscellaneous items which should be appended to *A Bibliography of Booth Tarkington*, edited by Russo and Sullivan.

SCOTT, JOHN D. "Tarkington and the 1920's." *American Scholar*, XXVI (Spring 1957), 181-94. Candid assessment of Tarkington in general, but mainly a strong defense of *Alice Adams* and its "sense of the small world." Peripheral comments often stimulating.

STREET, JULIAN. "When We Were Rather Young." *Saturday Evening Post,* CCV (August 20, 1932), 14-15+ and (November 19, 1932), 10-11+. Warmly personal reminiscences by a long-time friend and collaborator. Useful for insights into the personality of Tarkington.

VAN DOREN, CARL. *Contemporary American Novelists, 1900-1920.* New York: The Macmillan Company, 1922. Many judgments open to change since the study predates Tarkington's major works.

VAN NOSTRAND, ALBERT D. "The Novels and Plays of Booth Tarkington: A Critical Appraisal." Unpublished Ph.D. Dissertation, Harvard University, 1951. Elaborate analysis of relationships between Tarkington's novels and their dramatic adaptations. Excellent resource for references on American stage in Tarkington's time.

WERTENBAKER, CHARLES. "Booth Tarkington." *Life,* VII (September 4, 1939), 55-60. Tribute to Tarkington as "Dean of American Letters" on his seventieth birthday. Excellent comments on "professionalism" and the "successful" novelist.

WOODRESS, JAMES. *Booth Tarkington: Gentleman from Indiana.* New York: J. B. Lippincott Company, 1955. Possibly the last general biography of Tarkington—solid but not stodgy, thorough but not formidable.

—————. "Tarkington's New York Literary Debut: Letters Written to His Family in 1899." Princeton University Library *Chronicle,* XVI (Winter 1955), 54-79. Precisely what the title states, hence a convenient source of information on that chapter of Tarkington's career plus samples of his letter-writing style.

—————. "The Tarkington Papers." Princeton University Library *Chronicle,* XVI (Winter 1955), 45-53. Comprehensive description of the literary remains of Tarkington presented to his alma mater by Mrs. Tarkington. These papers constitute a major addition to the source material on contemporary American authors now available in various libraries.

WYATT, EDITH F. "Booth Tarkington: The Seven Ages of Man." *North American Review,* CCXVI (October 1922), 499-512. Forthright defense of Tarkington as mature artist. Perceptive analysis of the unifying philosophy through all his principal works.

# Index

90789

DATE D